ADVANCE PRAISE

Free Nurses is a powerful, no-fluff guide to creating the life nurses truly deserve. Mandie Jo blends financial education, real estate investing, and mindset mastery into a roadmap that's clear, actionable, and incredibly inspiring.

As someone who's passionate about nurses building generational wealth, I'm thrilled to see another resource that not only uplifts but equips nurses with the exact steps to create financial and personal freedom—on their own terms.

–Savannah Arroyo, RN, MSN
@networthnurse
www.TheNetworthNurse.com

"One nurse's financial independence is another nurse's power."

That's what pulses through these pages—not one-size-fits-all wisdom, but hard-won, real-world truth.

Mandie Jo writes from the perspective of a nurse who's lived it. She's survived on-the-job assault, rebuilt after a controlling relationship—and in this book, she brings it all into the light.

Her stories don't just resonate—they reflect. You'll see yourself in these pages. More importantly? You'll see a way forward.

What sets this book apart is how Mandie Jo draws a straight line between emotional trauma and financial behavior—with the precision of a mental health nurse and the clarity of someone who's come close to losing everything. This isn't surface-level advice. It's bedside grit turned into a blueprint.

As a nurse practitioner who made nursing work optional through a simple, repeatable money strategy, I know this deeply:

- Wealth isn't about math.
- It's saying no to dangerous shifts without spiraling.
- It's skipping overtime without second-guessing it.
- It's knowing your paycheck isn't your lifeline—because your plan is already doing the heavy lifting.
- It's working when you want—if you want.

Mandie Jo and I took different paths to financial freedom, but the truth is the same:

You can't afford to wait until you're broken to start thinking about what's next.

This book is an encouragement to get out ahead of what every nurse knows is coming—the physical and emotional exhaustion that makes this career unsustainable long-term.

That's not pessimism—it's reality. And because of that, you have to be intentional with your money now.

So you have options.

So you can choose.

That way, you can stop showing up as someone the system can discard, and start walking in as someone it can't afford to lose.

– Angel Mathis, MN, MPH, ARNP, RN, FNP-BC
Founder, Nurses Investing for Wealth®
Creator of the first State Board of Nursing–Approved Financial Literacy Program for Nurses
@nurseinvestingforwealth and www.freenurses.co/nifw

Mandie Jo doesn't just help nurses survive the system; she empowers them to rise above it and reclaim their freedom.

Free Nurses is a movement built on mindset mastery, financial literacy, and unstoppable momentum. But what truly sets it apart is Mandie herself.

I've had the honor of walking alongside her through our Invest Diva Accelerator and Triple Compounding journey, and I've seen firsthand the depth of her commitment, resilience, and heart.

If you're a new nurse feeling overwhelmed, underpaid, or unsure how to build a life you love, *Free Nurses* is the guide you didn't know you needed, and Mandie Jo is the mentor you've been waiting for.

She has a rare gift for making you feel seen, supported, and capable from the start. Mandie blends real-world strategy with deep compassion, showing you how to master your mindset, money, and momentum—so you don't just survive nursing, you thrive in it.

Starting strong with Mandie in your corner will change everything.

Mandie doesn't just want nurses to win; she wants them to experience true freedom personally, professionally, and financially. She has lived it, built it, and now leads others with clarity and compassion.

–Dr. Lisa Ballehr
www.drlisaballehr.com

As the Chief Financial Officer of a hospital, I have had the privilege of interacting with a wide array of professionals across healthcare, and I can confidently say that *Free Nurses* by Mandie Jo is an essential read for anyone in the healthcare field, especially nurses or those pursuing financial independence, regardless of their work field.

In an industry where burnout, long hours, and emotional labor can often overshadow personal financial well-being, this book provides a refreshing and practical approach to securing one's financial future.

The book is divided into clear, actionable steps that guide nurses through the often overwhelming landscape of financial independence. Mandie covers everything from budgeting and debt management to investment strategies and retirement planning. Each chapter is designed with a focus on simplicity, making complex financial concepts accessible without overwhelming the reader.

The real value of this book lies in its approach to empowering nurses to take control of their financial destinies. The author doesn't just present theoretical ideas—she provides real-world, actionable strategies that nurses can implement immediately.

What distinguishes this book from other general financial independence guides is its deeply personal approach to the nursing profession. It recognizes the financial strain that often comes with working in a field where the hours are long, the stress is high, and the rewards are, too often, intangible. By addressing these challenges head-on, the book provides the emotional and financial tools necessary to thrive in both personal and professional life.

Mandie's ability to speak to the emotional side of financial independence, especially the pressure to balance caregiving with self-care, is profound. Nurses often find themselves at the bottom of the priority list, and *Free Nurses* offers a refreshing shift in perspective, encouraging nurses to prioritize their financial security as a means of ensuring long-term well-being.

There are several key takeaways from the book that stood out to me as a healthcare executive:

1. The Power of Multiple Income Streams: Nurses, like many professionals, often rely on a single income. The book stresses the importance of diversifying income, whether through side gigs, real estate, or investments, which can significantly ease financial pressures and promote long-term security.

2. Understanding Healthcare Benefits: One of the book's strongest chapters is dedicated to helping nurses navigate the complex world of healthcare benefits—an area that many nurses, despite being healthcare experts, do not fully understand.

3. Mental and Emotional Clarity: Nurses, like other frontline workers, face unique stressors. The book touches

on the importance of having a clear financial vision in order to reduce financial anxiety and free up mental space to focus on patient care.

4. Legacy Planning and Family Security: In addition to building wealth, the book emphasizes planning for the future through wills, life insurance, and other forms of legacy planning—critical steps in securing a financial future for both the nurse and their family.

Free Nurses is more than just a financial guide—it is a much-needed resource for a group of professionals who often neglect their own financial security in the pursuit of caring for others. This book is an invaluable resource for nurses looking to take control of their financial future, and I highly recommend it not only for nurses but for anyone in the healthcare field who wishes to take charge of their financial health.

As a hospital CFO, I firmly believe that empowering nurses with the knowledge and tools to achieve financial independence will not only improve their personal lives but also enhance the overall care and outcomes we strive to deliver in healthcare.

–Troy E Eller, MBA
Chief Financial Officer
Hendry Regional Medical Center

FREE NURSES

Six Secrets to a Fabulous, Freakin' Good Nurse Life

MANDIE JO,
BSN, RN, PMH-BC, CARN

FREE NURSES

Six Secrets to a Fabulous, Freakin' Good Nurse Life

Special rates are available for educational institutions, nonprofit organizations, and hospitals, and bulk orders of 25 copies or more.

Mandie Jo is available for speaking engagements, workshops, and events focused on nursing empowerment, financial freedom, and mindset transformation. To book Mandie Jo or to inquire about bulk purchases of *Free Nurses* for your organization, school, or team, please contact:

✉ **mandie@thefreenurses.com**

ISBN: 979-8-9992030-4-5

Book Design by Transcendent Publishing | TranscendentPublishing.com
Edited by Mary Rembert
Author photography by Aleksandar Velickovic | @iamaleks94

The information provided in this book is for educational and informational purposes only and is not intended as medical, financial, or legal advice. While every effort has been made to ensure the accuracy of the content, the author and publisher make no representations or warranties regarding the completeness, accuracy, applicability, or suitability of the information contained herein.

This book is not a substitute for professional advice. Always seek the guidance of a qualified healthcare provider with any questions you may have regarding a medical condition, and consult a CPA before making any investment or financial decisions.

The author shares personal experiences and strategies that have worked for her, including in areas such as healthcare, real estate, investing, and entrepreneurship. Individual results may vary, and there are no guarantees of income, outcomes, or financial success. Any examples of earnings or investment returns are for illustrative purposes only and should not be considered typical or promised results.

The author and publisher disclaim any liability, loss, or risk incurred due to the use or application of any information contained in this book.

"The most revolutionary act one can commit
in our world is to be happy."

–Dr. Patch Adams

CONTENTS

Foreword xv

Introduction xvii

Chapter 1: Vision and Purpose 1

Chapter 2: The Power of Mentorship 39

Chapter 3: Financial Stability Through Home Ownership . 77

Chapter 4: Managing Finances 107

Chapter 5: Investing in the Stock Market 137

Chapter 6: Be Your Own Nurse Boss 161

The Nurse Freedom Formula 187

Acknowledgments 191

About the Author 193

DEDICATION

To all nurses who walk the fine line between science and art, whose every touch and thought carries the weight of compassion, whose tears and sweat carry the strength of care. May this book honor your dedication and inspire your journey toward freedom and happiness.

FOREWORD

When I first met Mandie Jo, I immediately knew she was different. Not just another nurse looking for a financial fix, but a woman with fire in her spirit, a deep passion for service, and an unstoppable vision for freedom. What started as a journey to secure her financial future evolved into a full-on revolution: one that's about to change YOUR life too.

Nurses are the backbone of healthcare—saving lives, soothing fears, and holding families together in the darkest hours. But who's been showing up to save the nurses? For far too long, nurses have been taught to survive paycheck to paycheck, work endless shifts, and sacrifice their dreams in the name of service.

Mandie Jo says: *No more.*

Free Nurses isn't just a book—it's financial CPR for the modern nurse. It's a permission slip to stop surviving and start thriving. It's a roadmap out of burnout, exhaustion, and feeling trapped, leading you into a life where you don't have to choose between your passion and your prosperity.

Mandie Jo walks the talk. She went from saving lives in the psych unit to saving her family's financial future, amassing a $1.3M net worth while still working as a nurse. She's built property portfolios, passive income streams, and a business—and she's doing it in scrubs and sneakers, not power suits and corner offices.

Inside these pages, you'll learn her VIPRN-Boss system:

- How to create a vision and purpose that pulls you forward
- How to invest wisely and build real wealth
- How to leverage property and real estate as passive income
- How to maximize your resources and finances
- How to find mentors and surround yourself with people who win
- How to become the boss of your life, not just an employee in someone else's empire.

In my world at Invest Diva, we talk a lot about financial empowerment and investing with confidence. Mandie Jo brings that same unstoppable energy to nurses, making it fun, simple, and incredibly powerful. She proves you don't need Wall Street suits or an MBA to achieve financial freedom. You just need a system, a little bit of faith, and a lot of fire.

So if you're tired of living shift to shift, tired of watching your dreams get postponed indefinitely, and tired of thinking financial freedom is for "someone else"—it's time.

Turn the page.

Read it.

Live it.

And never beg for a paycheck again.

Your future self will thank you.

–Kiana Danial
CEO of Invest Diva
Wall Street Journal Bestselling Author of *Million Dollar Family Secrets*

INTRODUCTION

Every day, nurses like us slip on our shoes, knowing we're walking into chaos but not knowing if we'll walk out okay. We face a choice. We can succumb to the exhausting demands of our profession or find a path leading to personal and professional liberation. Which choice have you made?

Are you a frustrated nurse or a free nurse?

Are you a fretting, fed-up nurse or a free nurse?

Are you burned out, need more money, or questioning why you ever became a nurse? Or are you a free nurse?

YOU MIGHT BE A FED-UP NURSE IF ...

- You've ever had a patient tell you, "You're just here for the paycheck," after they throw something at you.
- You check the clock 87 times between 7:00 and 7:14 a.m.
- The phrase "self-care" makes you want to throw your half-eaten protein bar across the breakroom.
- You've requested time off and still had to explain why you *need* a family vacation.
- You can spot a code brown from 30 feet away, but can't remember the last time you peed during your shift.

- You hear "staff meeting" and feel an instant spike in your cortisol.

- You've been told to "act like a professional" while someone screamed in your face.

- You've considered becoming a travel nurse, an Amazon driver, and a llama farmer all in the same week.

- Your paycheck disappears faster than your patience during a double shift.

- You've got a master's degree, a certification, and 14 years of experience—and still have to ask permission to change the temperature in the staff lounge.

- You've said, "I didn't go to nursing school for this" while untangling a patient from their IV pole, sock, and sense of vengeance.

- You've dreamt of walking out mid-shift and starting a goat sanctuary somewhere in the mountains.

- You know there *has* to be more to life than meds, madness, and mandatory overtime.

Fed-up nurses:

- Work more shifts than they want, driven out of fear or necessity.

- Constantly question their career choices, feeling stuck and unfulfilled.

- Feel burdened by systemic issues like staffing, blaming themselves, or the healthcare system or hospital.

- Sacrifice personal time, missing out on life's most important moments.

- Show up burnt out, dreaming of being anywhere but at work.

On the other hand, Free Nurses:

- Pursue their nursing careers confidently, anchored by a clear sense of purpose.
- Enjoy financial stability that empowers rather than confines. Their path grounds them.
- Use positive affirmations daily to maintain a mindset of abundance and resilience despite challenges and suffering.
- Spend as much time with their family and friends as they want while serving their patients and customers at the highest level.
- Manage challenges with courage, focusing on problems they can control.

Are you tired of being the fed-up nurse, doing more than your share, getting less recognition, and questioning whether this grind is really worth it? Are you ready to step into the shoes of a free nurse, where purpose, freedom, and fulfillment define your nursing career?

A NURSE'S JOURNEY TO FREEDOM

Hi, my name is Mandie Jo. I am a psychiatric mental health nurse from the beautiful town of Whitefish, Montana, close to Glacier National Park. With over 18 years of nursing experience and certified expertise in addictions and mental health, my professional journey has been as rewarding as it has been challenging. I continue to be amazed at how it reaches new heights.

In December 2022, amidst the global chaos of a pandemic and after the personal trials of managing as a clinical nurse leader during COVID, my life changed in one terrible moment when a patient assaulted me.

It wasn't the first time I had been assaulted, but this time I was left with a concussion, PTSD, and a cracked sense of reality.

But strangely, it also gave me clarity. This assault was not just a physical injury—it was a pivotal moment that forced me to reevaluate my life and my career.

Like many healthcare professionals, I entered this field driven by a calling—a deep-seated desire to help and heal. The day I was born, my father was a patient in the same hospital, battling a chronic autoimmune disorder. From as early as I can remember, hospitals were comforting places for me, filled with memories of playing, visiting, and hopefully waiting with my family for good news. This exposure set the stage for my nursing career, and I haven't looked back since.

Although most nurses question their career choices at some point, I have always been clear about my reasons for entering this profession. I've long believed that caring for others should not come at the expense of our well-being. Caring for others creates resilience, which provides renewed energy to keep going despite stressful and intense experiences.

Yet, I have witnessed nurses suffering from compassion fatigue and burnout time and time again, not fully understanding the reasons why. I've seen so many new graduates drop out of the profession within their first few years after spending four tireless years in college.

My grappling with these issues intensified after I was assaulted by said patient, prompting questions every nurse eventually faces:

What next?

Can I continue in this emotionally and physically draining profession?

Is this the end of my career?

What if I can't return to nursing as I know it?

What if I need a secondary income because I can't work as much?

What if I were so injured on the job that I had to switch professions completely?

These questions threw me off balance, but did not diminish my passion for nursing; instead, they redirected my focus toward discovering and creating a sustainable life that nurtures both my professional ambitions and personal well-being. It fueled my desire to help nurses find their freedom.

After all, I am a nurse through and through, and I recognize that society fundamentally relies on nurses to function. The nursing shortage is palpable to patients and staff, and we need more nurses, not less. So, how can we keep nurses in the field and increase the number of practicing nurses while ensuring they can practice with as little worry, fear, and pain as possible? This journey defines the steps to becoming a "free nurse."

What exactly is a "free nurse"? Being a free nurse means caring for patients at the highest level without sacrificing one's own health. It means working as little or as much as you want. While you are being paid for your highest level of service, there is no pressure to work to care for your family. You work because you love it, and the financial stress doesn't come with it. Sounds impossible, right?

Did you know that Florence Nightingale, often considered the founder of modern nursing and our ultimate role model, came from a wealthy upper-class British family? Her family's wealth provided her with financial security, allowing her to pursue her interests in nursing and healthcare reform without the need to work for a living.

This financial independence was crucial, enabling her to focus on her pioneering work in nursing, hospital sanitation, healthcare reform, and statistics without the economic pressures many of her contemporaries faced.

Nightingale's background significantly influenced her ability to influence healthcare practices and policies effectively. Her secure financial situation allowed her the freedom to travel, study, and implement her ideas, which might have been considerably more challenging without such economic stability.

It's time to return to the days of Florence Nightingale (with a little more advancement and technology, of course)—A life where you have a secure income. No more burnout, compassion fatigue, or working under compulsion. Can you imagine?

Nursing is hard enough without all that other stuff. When hospitals employ free nurses, patient outcomes will improve, just like they did for Florence.

Let's take it a step further . . .

IMAGINE THIS: WHAT HAPPENS WHEN NURSES OWN THE SYSTEM?

It's 2035. And something remarkable has happened. Nurses don't just clock in and out anymore—they call the shots. Literally.

It started with just a few. A nurse in Florida opened a recovery home for young adults transitioning out of psychiatric care. One in Atlanta launched a holistic clinic that combined trauma-informed care with yoga and nutrition coaching. A night-shift ICU nurse in Seattle created an app that helps new nurses manage their time, chart faster, and sleep better.

And then it spread—like wildfire, only healing.

Before long, nurses weren't just following orders. They were founding companies. Designing systems. Investing in communities. Teaching others how to live, not just patch things up.

Everywhere you look, something has changed:

Hospitals run more efficiently. Nurses opened consulting firms, advising on policy and workflow, not just nursing ratios. They understood how hospitals function as businesses because they owned their own businesses.

Healthcare startups flourish. Nurses were building tools that worked for real people. No more apps that didn't speak nursing language or charting software that felt like punishment.

Workplaces are safer and the staff are better paid. Nurse CEOs prioritized mental health, equity, and respect. They weren't afraid to say, "No, that's not good enough." There were more nurses, so they could focus on their side hustles and work shifts with ratios that were sustainable.

Communities are healthier. Nurses opened wellness clinics, group homes, mobile mental health units, lactation consulting practices, and grief retreats.

Nursing students dream bigger. They see what is possible. They aren't stuck in "bedside or burnout" anymore. They have mentors who teach them how to budget, build a business, and lead with heart.

And what's more?

Patients are hopeful. Because for the first time in history, the people with the most hands-on experience in healing are finally leading the charge, not just participating in someone else's vision.

Nurses didn't leave nursing.

They changed it.

Here's the exciting part about this story! It's already happening.

My mission is to serve nurses at the highest level so they can achieve financial, mental, and physical health and freedom. This freedom will allow them to work as much or as little as they want, to be at the bedside with a caring, altruistic approach without the shadow of financial worries, to focus on their families, and to fulfill their given or chosen purpose in life, which may or may not be nursing. (That's right, nurses should and do have a life outside of nursing, which can fuel their passion even more for nursing!)

My more altruistic and lofty vision—my "giraffe" goal, as my mentor Kiana Danial would call it—is to solve the nursing shortage. When all nurses are free nurses, more will join the ranks!

The sooner nurses can achieve this freedom, the sooner our hospitals will be staffed safely, patient outcomes will improve, and nurses and their families will be healthy and happy. At least one problem off the world stage! There, I spoke it into the universe; it shall be done.

This book, *Free Nurses*, is born from these experiences and aspirations. It is designed to guide nurses and healthcare professionals—and maybe even hospital administrators suffering from nurse shortages—through crafting a life for a nurse who is devoted to serving others and achieving personal happiness, health, and financial freedom.

Through the six steps outlined in this book—from creating a vision board to building a business and investing—I aim to share the lessons I've learned and the strategies that have helped me build a life in which I can choose how much or how little I wish to work while serving my community at the highest level.

As we delve into these steps, I hope you will find inspiration and practical advice to take charge of your journey toward freedom and fulfillment. Happy nursing and happy investing in yourself, your freedom, and your future!

CHAPTER 1

VISION AND PURPOSE

Myth #1:
There is such a thing as work-life balance.

She wasn't famous. She didn't have a book deal or a million followers on Instagram. She wasn't a Chief Nursing Officer, either. She was a floor nurse—BSN, RN, two certifications, three kids, one aging parent, and a heart so big it practically walked into the room before she did.

She worked night shift because the pay was better and the house was quieter during the day. She clocked in tired but determined, her badge dragging behind her like a cape that had been washed too many times.

This nurse didn't want much. Just a decent ratio, safe staffing, and a shift where no one screamed, bled, coded, or cried in the breakroom. She wanted to go home before the sun came up and feel like her work mattered. But every month, the bills piled up, and the exhaustion crept in.

She thought about going back to school—again. Maybe this time it would pay off. Maybe this time the debt would be worth it. Or maybe she'd feel more trapped, behind, and burned out.

Then one day, in a quiet moment between med passes and admissions, she had a thought.

What if she didn't need *more credentials*—what if she needed more **control**?

What if she could still be a nurse … but also an investor?

A homeowner?

A business owner?

A nurse with savings, vision, and a plan?

What if she could heal others without destroying herself?

This nurse didn't quit nursing. She simply decided to stop *bleeding for it*. She started making her money work for her. She stopped apologizing for wanting time off. She stopped pretending that a hospital paycheck was the only way she could serve others.

She built a life where she could practice from purpose, not pressure.

This, dear reader, is a modern-day Florence Nightingale. Not an icon on a pedestal. Just a nurse like you—learning how to be *free*.

THE SECRET NO ONE HAS TOLD YOU

Let me tell you a secret: work–life balance is a lie. And believing in it might be why you're still burnt out, broke, or questioning your entire nursing career. When I hear someone say they need more work–life balance, it is often code for "I don't like my life, I'm working too much, I'm not happy with the work I do."

Or perhaps someone else is telling this person to work less, get their priorities straight, and quit focusing on money or job satisfaction. Listen, plenty of people are working 60–70–80 hours a week doing things they love, getting paid or not getting paid, even while not missing out on the other things in life they love too. They spend time with their family when they want, perhaps even involving their family in their purpose, mission, and work. They are not generally neglectful.

So, is there an erroneous belief that work–life balance will make one happier? Yes. In reality, there is no such thing as work–life balance, and pursuing it is just what many big businesses, like hospitals or unions, want from you. Why?

A little history of work–life balance might clarify things. The term "work–life balance" originated in the mid-20th century, reflecting a growing awareness of the need for a healthy balance between work responsibilities and personal life. It became more prominent during the 1970s and 1980s as changes in work patterns, societal expectations, and gender roles increased the focus on balancing career and family life.

Originally, the concept was often discussed in the context of women's rights and the challenges working mothers faced in juggling employment with family obligations. Over time, the discussion expanded to include men and the broader work-force, recognizing that achieving a satisfactory balance between work demands and personal life is a common struggle for many people, regardless of gender.

The increasing interest in work-life balance was also driven by research showing that prolonged work stress and poor balance can negatively affect personal health, job performance, and overall life satisfaction. This awareness led to more discussions on flexible work arrangements, mental health, and the importance of leisure and family time, shaping the modern understanding of work-life balance as essential for well-being and productivity.

SEEKING WORK-LIFE BALANCE IS A LIMITING BELIEF

From my mental health nurse perspective, encouraging others to seek work-life balance is healthy. However, seeking work-life balance can be a limiting belief because it does not consider YOUR vision for life! If your vision and mission are clear, you don't care how much time you spend on your work. You can't wait to wake up and do more of it!

Before we dive deeper into the myths around work-life balance, let me share a moment from my own life when this concept shattered for me—in the best possible way.

Like many nurses (and high-achievers in general), I spent years trying to "balance" everything, often wondering if something was wrong with me for wanting more. But one pivotal decision at a young age—and a simple sentence from a mentor much later in life—changed how I saw everything.

The Day I Knew Work-Life Balance Was a Lie

It was my senior year of high school, and I had told my school counselor all year long that I wasn't going to college. Nope. Not doing it. College felt like a scam, a racket. It didn't align with my goals, especially my desire to go into full-time missionary work.

I wasn't interested in student loan debt, dorm rooms, or degrees that didn't move the needle on my purpose. And then one day, without warning, I walked into her office and told her I had changed my mind.

I still remember the look on her face. She was elated, but so confused.

I wasn't confused, though; everything in me clicked. I realized that nursing could be the bridge between my goals: serving others, supporting my family, staying intrigued with life, and funding my missions.

I knew I had to move fast. I only had a few weeks to get my college application in. But that's how I work. When my purpose aligns, I don't waste time, and I don't think I'm unique here.

I didn't just go to nursing school—I went all in. I took a part-time job in the scholarship department at the university, dedicated 70 hours a month to mission work, and still showed up to class ready to learn. I found creative ways to fund school and walked away with only $17,000 in loans and a four-year degree. That was the start of a pattern I've lived ever since.

But here's the thing: people have told me I was doing too much my entire life. They asked, "How can you juggle all of this? Why can't you slow down?"

For a long time, I wondered if they were right. Was something wrong with me? Why didn't I crave rest the way others seemed to? Why did I always have a new plan, idea, or goal to chase down?

It wasn't until my mentor casually said one day, "There's no such thing as work-life balance" that everything shifted. The shame I carried for being "too much" lifted at that moment. I realized I wasn't broken. I was aligned.

Balance isn't about doing less. It's about aligning your life so beautifully that everything you do—from your work to your family to your goals—flows together like a masterpiece. Balance isn't hours on a clock; it's harmony in your purpose. And for me, purpose means waking up every day with an idea I can't wait to pursue.

That conversation with my mentor rewired something in me. I stopped chasing balance and started building alignment. And that's what I want for you, too. Not a perfectly divided pie chart of life, but a vision that is so clear and purpose-driven that everything you do fuels everything else. I believe that this is what everyone is seeking. It's not less work. It's the freedom to build your life on your terms.

WHAT DOES WORK-LIFE FREEDOM *ACTUALLY* LOOK LIKE?

Forget hustle culture and burnout memes for a second—what if working hard didn't mean being miserable? What if "doing the most" actually felt *energizing* because you loved what you were doing? What if freedom wasn't about quitting ... but *choosing*?

Before we dig into the practical steps of becoming a Free Nurse, let's pause for a reality check: What does *loving your work* actually look like in real life? And is it possible to *work hard and still feel free*?

Whether you're a bedside warrior, a clinic queen, or a nurse leader trying to stay afloat, chances are you've been told to "slow down," "get balance," or "stop working so much." But what if work doesn't *have* to feel like work? What if freedom isn't about working less—it's about doing work that lights you up?

Here are a few inspiring figures—nurse and non-nurse—who have crafted lives of purpose, passion, and power. Some are legends. Some are controversial. But they all chose work that felt deeply aligned with their mission and values.

Let's take a look ...

Elon Musk

The CEO of Tesla and SpaceX, Elon Musk, is known for his intense work ethic, reportedly working between 80 and 100 hours a week. Despite this demanding schedule, Musk expresses extreme enthusiasm for his projects, which aim to revolutionize transportation on Earth and in space. He says, "If something is important enough, even if the odds are against you, you should still do it."[1] Elon has managed to father 11 children by age 52, so you can't tell me he isn't at least

---

[1] Elon Musk, "Interview with Scott Pelley," YouTube Video, 2012, *60 Minutes, CBS News*, https://youtu.be/23GzpbNUyI4

somewhat interested in family life. He certainly has the means to care for them financially. Regardless of your opinion of him, his values, decisions, or political views, you must admit he enjoys his work!

Martha Stewart

Before becoming a media mogul, Martha Stewart built a catering business that demanded long hours and hard work. Her dedication expanded into various business ventures, including television shows, books, and merchandise.

Despite the demands, Stewart has always seemed to thrive on her busy schedule and diverse business activities. She didn't start her first business until the age of 50! She recently purchased property with her daughter. Yes, she's been in jail, however, she still knows how to live a life she enjoys despite her criminal history and past mistakes, which she has capitalized on.

Lisa Nichols

Lisa is a phenomenal example of turning adversity into abundance. She went from being a single mom on public assistance with $11 in the bank to becoming a millionaire entrepreneur and one of the most sought-after motivational speakers in the world.

She famously said, "I had to be willing to completely die to any form of me that I had been, so that I could birth the woman that I was becoming."[2] Her energy is contagious, and her story is a masterclass in grit, faith, and massive action.

---

[2] "Caption, Subtitle and Translate Video," amara, accessed May 12, 2025, https://amara.org/videos/uE2kB5RoHuah/en/2793188/?utm_source=chatgpt.com.

Lisa is a *New York Times* bestselling author and one of only two Black women to take her company, Motivating the Masses Inc., public.

Mother Teresa

Mother Teresa received numerous awards for her work, including the Nobel Peace Prize in 1979. Despite facing criticism and challenges, she remained committed to her mission until her health declined. She passed away in 1997 but left behind a legacy of compassion and service that continues to inspire millions worldwide. Her life exemplifies how deeply fulfilling it can be to dedicate oneself completely to a cause, particularly when driven by strong faith and a commitment to serve others.

Mother Teresa and her sisters started their day at 4:30 a.m. with prayers and Mass, followed by a day of service. They cared for the sick, the dying, and orphans and ran soup kitchens, mobile clinics, and schools.

Her "balance" was less about dividing time between personal life and work and more about integrating her calling into every aspect of her existence, finding joy and satisfaction in the love and service she extended to others. Though not called a nurse, she was the essence of a nurse!

Taylor Swift

As of October 2024, *Forbes* reported that Taylor Swift's net worth had reached $1.6 billion, making her the world's wealthiest female musician at that time.[3] This valuation reflects her suc-

---

[3] Conor Murray. "Taylor Swift Becomes World's Richest Female Musician—Here's Who Is Right Behind Her," *Forbes*, 8 Oct. 2024, https://www.forbes.com/sites/conormurray/2024/10/08/taylor-swift-becomes-worlds-richest-female-musician-heres-who-is-right-behind-her

cess across multiple aspects of her career, including album sales, tours, endorsements, and various other business ventures. Swift has been consistently recognized as one of the highest-earning musicians in the world, with her tours and music releases contributing significantly to her financial success.

Taylor Swift's ability to work long hours while enjoying her life stems from her profound passion for her craft and her commitment to her fans. Her career provides her with a creative outlet and a means to connect deeply with audiences worldwide, making the hard work and long hours worthwhile.

"This is the proudest and happiest I've ever felt, and the most creatively fulfilled and free I've ever been," Taylor says. And, of course, we know Taylor has a pretty active social life; we see it in the news almost every day and sometimes at football games!

Florence Nightingale

Known for her work during the Crimean War and beyond, Florence Nightingale's relentless work ethic was fueled by a strong sense of duty and care for the well-being of soldiers and patients. Beyond her nursing duties, Nightingale was a skilled statistician who used her knowledge to argue for hospital reform. Yes, dear nurses, the need for hospital reform is nothing new.

She founded the Nightingale School of Nursing at St. Thomas' Hospital in London, the first secular nursing school in the world, and wrote extensively on health, medicine, and nursing. "I attribute my success to this: I never gave or took any excuse," she famously said.[4] This quote reflects her no-nonsense

---

[4] Edward Cook, *The Life of Florence Nightingale, by Sir Edward Cook*, (London: Macmillan, 1913).

approach to her work and her relentless pursuit of improvements in healthcare, regardless of the obstacles she faced. Florence also never had children and was never married, which was very controversial for a woman then.

Warren Buffett

Warren Buffett, chairman and CEO of Berkshire Hathaway, is one of the most iconic investors in the world. Even in his 90s, Buffett still went to work every day—not because he had to, but because he genuinely enjoyed it. Known for his humility, long-term thinking, and famously frugal lifestyle, Buffett often emphasizes that doing what you love every day is one of the keys to a successful life.

He once said, "We have long had jobs that we love, in which we are helped in countless ways by talented and cheerful associates. Every day is exciting to us; no wonder we tap-dance to work."[5]

That simple phrase reveals everything about his mindset: he doesn't see work as a burden. He sees it as joy.

Buffett also believes in the power of compounding—of money, yes, but also of habits, learning, and consistency. His continued passion for his craft, even after building an empire worth over $100 billion, is a masterclass in loving what you do and never stopping learning.

UNIQUENESS AND VISION

All these individuals have something in common—they are unique, and their vision defines their work and life, even if they

---

[5] Shareholder letters, accessed May 27, 2025, https://www.berkshirehathaway.com/letters/letters.html.

are no longer alive. Their purpose is that powerful! And what makes them even more unique? There was only one of them! No one else can or could do what they do or did.

Now, if that isn't a staffing shortage, I don't know what is! They faced being pulled in multiple directions and sometimes lacked the support they wanted every day. Yet, they thrived because their work aligned with their deeper purpose and vision.

As nurses, if we can individually define our vision and align our work with our core values and passions, the concept of work-life balance shifts. It becomes about integration and fulfillment rather than a strict division between work and personal life.

Do you connect with or admire any one of these individuals? What individual do you admire? Identifying these individuals tells you much about your work and life views. And how might this shift a negative view of lack and shortage to one of opportunities and possibilities?

Brian Cerezo, The Money Nurse, whom I had the honor of interviewing, views time management and work–life balance with a pragmatic and disciplined approach. Brian is a savvy investor and podcast host. His YouTube channel, *Direct Admission*, dives deep into the various opportunities for nurses to augment their income, from side hustles to sophisticated investment strategies like options trading. He recently launched a course specifically designed to teach nurses the ins and outs of options trading. He is also a nurse millionaire!

Brian emphasizes communication and collaboration with his family, particularly with his wife, to make his busy schedule work. "For my podcast, I could only record on Sundays.

That's the day that my wife and I talked about it. We're just like, Sunday mornings are great to do it. The kids are going to play with each other until 12 noon," Brian explained. He maximizes that time by recording longer-form content; for shorter content, he works during quieter moments when his kids are asleep.

Brian also shared insights from one of his podcast guests, explaining how they, too, found time for content creation. "He'll set aside three to four hours to record as many reels and TikToks as he possibly can and then just schedule them out for two or three weeks in advance."

Brian applies a similar method, acknowledging that time is limited but achievable when you are passionate about your work. His key takeaway for balancing work, family, and entre-preneurship is straightforward: "You just gotta do it. No one cares if you're tired." We're not encouraging lack of sleep here, but rather a passion for your work that makes it hard to sleep because you are excited for what lies ahead!

WHAT YOU DON'T NEED

What these individuals do not have in common, which addresses another limiting belief, is access to resources and upbringing. Most, like Buffett, Cerezo, Musk, Nichols, and Stewart, built their fortunes from more modest beginnings through their entrepreneurial efforts.

Others, like Swift and Nightingale, benefited from their family's financial stability, which provided a platform from which they could launch their careers. Mother Teresa, however, chose a path that eschewed personal wealth entirely. Each path highlights different ways financial backgrounds can shape, but not necessarily determine, personal and career outcomes.

Where does this take you? It all depends on what you truly want!

In the next section, we'll explore how to create a vision board to help clarify your goals and align your daily actions with your ultimate aspirations, setting a foundation for becoming a free nurse!

MEET SARAH: THE "GOOD NURSE" WHO WAS QUIETLY FALLING APART

Sarah had been an ER nurse for 15 years. She was damn good at her job—quick on her feet, calm during codes, and always the first to volunteer for the worst shifts.

Patients loved her. Doctors respected her. Management trusted her.

But Sarah was quietly unraveling.

Her back hurt. Her marriage was tense. Her checking account looked like a flatline most months. Her kids told her she was "never home." And her Sunday nights were haunted by the same thought, over and over again:

"I don't think I can keep doing this."

So she tried to fix it the way most nurses do—by rearranging her schedule, taking a yoga class, downloading a mindfulness app, maybe switching to a different department. She even flirted with the idea of going back to school.

But nothing stuck. Because all those strategies were surface-level, and the problem wasn't surface-level.

The problem was this: Sarah didn't have a vision. She had a job.

She'd built her entire life around surviving the next shift instead of building a future she actually wanted. And no amount of yoga or PTO was going to fix that.

Everything changed when she heard someone say, "There's no such thing as work-life balance—only alignment."

It hit her like an IV push of epinephrine.

She didn't need to slow down. She needed to aim differently. She needed to make her work *work for her.*

So Sarah made a decision.

She created a vision board—not just of her dream vacation or ideal home—but of her values. Her future self. Her legacy. She started learning about passive income. She found a nurse mentor who had retired *from the bedside* but not from her calling.

She stopped feeling guilty for wanting more.

Today, Sarah is still a nurse—but now it's on *her* terms. She works part-time, earns full-time income from a side business, and teaches other nurses how to build a life they don't need to escape.

She's no longer a nurse on the brink. She's a free nurse.

CREATING A VISION BOARD

If you're still chasing balance, I dare you to stop. Chase alignment instead—and watch what happens.

Start now with a vision board, a powerful tool for visualizing your aspirations and goals. A vision board serves as a daily reminder and motivator by displaying your dreams, helping you stay focused on your ultimate aspirations.

At a more spiritual and cognitive level, vision boards invoke something ethereal: the power of thoughts and beliefs. Through my experiences, three tools have profoundly impacted my belief systems: the Bible, Cognitive Behavioral Therapy (CBT), and Rhonda Byrne's *The Secret*. With these three tools, I provide a starting point for a vision board. Stick with me here; I promise it stays real!

SPIRITUALITY AND VISION

This is not a religious book, of course, but discussing purpose, vision, and connection to something greater than ourselves inevitably touches on spirituality.

The relationship between nursing and religion can be traced back to various religious orders that emphasized caring for the sick as part of their spiritual practice.

For instance, Florence Nightingale felt called by God to her nursing career, which she infused with her spiritual values, viewing it as a divine calling to help those in need.

For 11 years, I lived my life on a mission—literally. Not the kind where you clock in at a hospital or clinic. Not the kind where you're rewarded with a paycheck or a plaque on the wall. It was a mission fueled purely by purpose and my nursing salary.

Each day, I stepped into the homes of people whose lives were unraveling. I provided mental health support, delivered meals, created social connections, and offered Bible education—all for free. No one was paying me. The congregation I was connected with didn't fund me. I wasn't sponsored. I was there because I believed in something bigger than myself: the transformative power of belief.

I often considered it a kind of "home health nursing," but it was even deeper than that. I wasn't just checking vital signs or handing out food, I was handing out hope. I was offering people a new belief system. An explanation for their suffering. A reason to wake up the next morning. A reason to believe that their future could still be different.

And isn't that what every human is ultimately searching for? A framework to make sense of their struggles—and a future worth moving toward.

At its core, this is why religions, spiritualities, and belief systems persist. They provide a scaffolding—a blueprint—for why life happens the way it does.

Sometimes these frameworks are empowering. Sometimes they can be dangerously limiting. But one thing is certain: they shape us all, whether we realize it or not.

You did not choose your earliest belief systems. They were given to you. They were programmed into your mind when you were most vulnerable and least questioning. And whether you've accepted, rejected, or redefined those beliefs, they've left their fingerprints on your mind and your future.

There's no judgment here. But if you want a different future, you must be brave enough to examine the frameworks you've inherited and consciously decide what to build next.

That's why belief is so central to this journey you're on right now. That's why building a vision board, casting a new future, and becoming a Free Nurse begins with your mind—not your money. Until you install new beliefs, you'll keep living out old, invisible scripts you didn't even write.

Even today, when people think about nurses, they aren't just thinking about technical skills. They are thinking about hope. Relief. Compassion. A reason to fight for one more day.

Nurses symbolize something ancient and universal: freedom from pain, intelligence and healing, and an unwavering belief that things can—and will—get better. Did you know you carry that power for others?

Religions gave us frameworks. Nursing gave us frameworks. Now it's time for you to create your own. That brings us to something I believe every nurse—and every human—should understand: **Cognitive behavioral therapy**.

Why? Because CBT is all about *beliefs*. It's the practical, evidence-based way to uncover the thoughts and patterns that drive your behavior—and more importantly, to change them.

COGNITIVE BEHAVIORAL THERAPY (CBT)

If you've ever found yourself stuck in a cycle—spending money you don't have, staying in a job that drains you, feeling like you'll never "get ahead," there's probably a hidden belief running the show. CBT helps you hold those thoughts up to the light, question them, and swap them out for something that serves the life you want to live.

Just like religion or nursing give us a framework for helping others, CBT gives us a framework for helping ourselves.

It's one of the most powerful tools I've ever used—and in the next few paragraphs, I'll show you exactly how it works and how you can use it to free your mind and build the future you *really* believe in.

Cognitive Behavioral Therapy (CBT) is a form of psychotherapy that emphasizes changing unhelpful cognitive distortions and behaviors to improve emotional regulation and develop effective coping strategies. I first learned about CBT when I began my mental health nursing journey, and I ate it up. Most mental health therapy today is based on CBT, which was developed in the 1960s, primarily by Dr. Aaron T. Beck and Dr. Albert Ellis.

- Albert Ellis developed Rational Emotive Behavior Therapy (REBT) in the 1950s, an early form of CBT influenced by Stoic philosophy. He focused on changing irrational beliefs that cause emotional distress.

- Aaron T. Beck developed cognitive therapy, now known as CBT, while researching depression. He identified "automatic thoughts"—negative and unrealistic thoughts that contribute to emotional difficulties. Beck's method involved identifying, challenging, and replacing these thoughts with more realistic interpretations.

CBT integrates behavioral techniques and is evidence-based and extensively tested across various psychological disorders. It has evolved to include third-wave therapies like Dialectical Behavior Therapy (DBT) and Acceptance and Commitment

Therapy (ACT), incorporating mindfulness and acceptance strategies.

This adaptability makes CBT a widely used and effective therapeutic approach in mental health. CBT's effectiveness in changing thoughts to influence emotions and behaviors can be powerfully applied in creating and utilizing vision boards. Here's the science behind how CBT principles enhance the vision board process, because we nurses just don't accept something without the facts:

- **Identifying and Modifying Beliefs:** CBT helps identify and challenge limiting beliefs that may hinder goal achievement. By incorporating affirmations and positive imagery that align with new, constructive beliefs, your vision board can transform these into daily reminders to reinforce positive thinking and behavior.

- **Behavioral Activation:** This CBT technique involves taking actions likely to lead to positive emotional states. By using your vision board to plan and visualize concrete steps toward your goals, you stimulate proactive behaviors each day.

- **Cognitive Rehearsal:** Regularly visualizing successful outcomes as depicted on your vision board can prepare you mentally to handle challenges and enhance resilience. This mental practice is a form of rehearsal that strengthens the neural pathways associated with successful behaviors and outcomes.

Okay, now to the good stuff, and unbeknownst to you, we have already done several CBT interventions in this book on you, one of them is calling out a very common myth that might be limiting your full potential.

You may now be convinced that work-life balance is not a real thing, not one that would bring you what you really want. And so nothing can come in your way of being that free nurse—not staffing shortages, working long hours, your current financial situation, or family obligations. All challenges and seeming lack can be used to your advantage to build your vision board.

THE LAW OF ATTRACTION AND PRACTICAL STEPS

I remember learning about *The Secret* when it was first released and chalking it up to nothing more than a fantasy. I was encouraged to watch the documentary by my mentor, Kiana Danial, CEO of Invest Diva, when I enrolled in her Triple Compounding System, a rapid investing education and financial literacy course.

I enrolled soon after the assault happened, so it may have been the timing in my life, but this time, *The Secret* pulled me in like a little girl in a shop window.

The Secret by Rhonda Byrne is a self-help book that became a global phenomenon after its release in 2006. The book and subsequent film of the same name focus on the law of attraction or the law of love, which states that people can attract whatever they focus on into their lives through the power of their thoughts and emotions.

Rhonda Byrne was inspired to create *The Secret* after reading Wallace D. Wattles' book *The Science of Getting Rich,* which promotes the idea that positive thinking can attract wealth. After experiencing personal and professional challenges, Byrne discovered the law of attraction, which she credits with transforming her life.

The Secret and the law of attraction emphasize the power of positive thoughts to bring about positive experiences. This concept complements CBT by fostering an optimistic mindset essential for personal transformation.

I've watched the documentary at least 20 times, and Rhonda Byrne has a plethora of books and videos on YouTube. I've been surprised how much of it is also rooted in my Christian beliefs and uses CBT! It fed my fascination with belief and thought creation and helped me improve my ability to change negative thought patterns, which left me anxious, scared, and stuck. Her core principles provide a kick-ass start to behavioral change primarily because they are simple.

This approach ensures that your vision board is not just a tool for daydreaming (although daydreaming is highly encouraged when creating a vision board) but a catalyst for real action and achievement.

Here's how to harness the law of attraction in your vision board:

- **Visualization:** When you look at your vision board, imagine living out those successes and experiences. Visualization is a key technique in *The Secret* and involves deeply imagining achieving your goals. Feel the emotions as if you have already accomplished them.

This emotional resonance is said to increase the likelihood of these aspirations manifesting in your life.

- **Affirmations:** Alongside images, include positive affirmations on your vision board that reinforce your goals. Phrases like "I am successful," "I achieve my goals with ease," and "I am a committed and compassionate nurse" help solidify your intentions and keep your thoughts aligned with your desires.

- **Taking Action:** Set clear, achievable goals based on the visuals of your vision board. Ask yourself daily what small steps you can take to progress toward these goals. Stay open and receptive to opportunities that can move you closer to your aspirations.

- **Belief:** As stated in *The Secret*, belief is crucial for the law of attraction to work. Believe in the possibility of achieving what's on your vision board. Trust that the universe will align the opportunities and resources needed to achieve your dreams. This belief should be unwavering and act as a driving force in your daily actions and decisions.

Understanding and applying the principles from Rhonda Byrne's *The Secret*, specifically the law of attraction, can enhance the effectiveness of your vision board. Combining positive thinking with consistent action will motivate you and help you manifest your goals into reality. Remember, a vision board reflects your desires and a map to achieving them—engage with it actively and watch your dreams start to take shape.

COMPREHENSIVE GUIDE TO CREATING AND BUILDING A VISION BOARD

Step 1: Define Your Goals

Start by reflecting deeply on what you truly desire in both your personal and professional life. Use CBT to identify negative beliefs and the Law of Attraction to focus on positive outcomes.

- Example: If your goal is to advance in your nursing career to get a higher degree, write down specific aspects of this goal. Reflect on any doubts or fears about your qualifications and actively replace these thoughts with positive affirmations.

Step 2: Gather Inspiration

Collect images, quotes, and symbols that inspire and embody your aspirations. Choose visuals that resonate with your emotions and reflect the positive outcomes you envision through the Law of Attraction.

- Example: To help you achieve your goal of becoming a nurse manager, you might include pictures of inspiring leaders, symbols of leadership like a gavel or an emblem, and quotes from respected figures in the field.

Step 3: Choose a Board

Decide whether you prefer a physical board you can touch and see in your daily environment or a digital board for convenience and flexibility. Consider which form will make you feel more connected to your goals.

Step 4: Arrange and Attach

Organize your materials in a way that pleases you aesthetically and logically. Group similar goals together and use lines or arrows to connect related ideas, enhancing the flow of your board's layout.

Step 5: Strategic Placement

Place your vision board where you will see it every day, such as near your bed, at your desk, or as a background on your devices. The constant visibility will reinforce your goals and keep you motivated.

- Example: I have two boards, one physical board that is in my living room and one electronic board that is in a Google document. The Google document is easy to change; I can cut and paste pictures easily and recreate my future story as I see fit. I can access it from any mobile device, making it perfect for work and travel. My physical board is almost more of a "win" board now. It has thank you cards, mementos, words of encouragement, and tons of affirmations that others have given me. It reminds me of all the support I have and has so many affirmations and manifestations that are now a reality for me. This helps with my gratitude and reminds me that this stuff works.

Step 6: Behavioral Activation

Use the board as a daily reminder to engage in behaviors that progress toward your goals. Ensure it includes action-oriented images depicting the steps needed to achieve these goals.

- Example: If your personal goal is to improve your health, include a monthly checklist of measurable activities such as completing a certain number of workouts or preparing healthy meals, and visualize yourself achieving these.

Step 7: Update Regularly

Update your vision board as your goals evolve or you achieve certain milestones. This can be a rewarding activity that renews your motivation and adapts to your changing aspirations.

Step 8: Cognitive Rehearsal and Positive Self-Talk

Spend time each day practicing cognitive rehearsal by visualizing successful outcomes and overcoming potential obstacles. Accompany this practice with positive self-talk affirmations to strengthen your mental resilience.

- Example: I start each morning with a routine, which I will share, that gets me started for the day.

Step 9: Encourage Positive Self-Talk

Regularly engage with positive affirmations on your board to encourage a supportive and optimistic internal dialogue, which is essential for maintaining motivation and resilience against challenges.

By integrating CBT techniques, the law of attraction, and practical steps for creating a vision board, you create a dynamic tool that not only motivates but also strategically aligns your thoughts and behaviors toward achieving your desired outcomes.

This holistic approach ensures that your vision board is not just a collection of images but a catalyst for real and meaningful change, supporting your journey toward personal and professional fulfillment as a free nurse.

In the next section, we will explore establishing a morning routine that sets the tone for success and how this routine can further enhance the effectiveness of your vision board.

MORNING ROUTINE

Working on a psychiatric unit will teach you a few things very quickly:

One: You never know what's coming.

Two: You should always carry an extra set of scrubs.

Three: Your morning routine better be bulletproof—or you're not making it past breakfast.

In my time on the unit, I've had a woman use her bra as a slingshot. (Her aim was disturbingly good.)

I've met Jesus. I've met Buddha. I've even met the President— *multiple times.*

I've discovered that I apparently have a *lot* of friends in the CIA, according to several patients. (Honestly, it's flattering.)

I've been *built into* patients' video games as a character, which, depending on the day, was either a hero or the final boss they had to defeat.

I've watched patients stuff hospital-donated socks up their noses (a generous donation I now deeply regret).

I've walked in on more suicide attempts than I can count, usually armed with nothing but a clipboard and sheer nerve.

I've had bodily fluids from all sources on me—and no, I still don't know how they got there.

I've been locked inside a room by a patient who wanted a "private conversation" I definitely did not RSVP for.

And I've had to place more patients in restraints than Hugh Hefner has ever done to his Playboy Bunnies.

The sheer insanity I have purposely placed myself in—and somehow not been sucked into—sometimes amazes even me.

And that's just psych nursing.

Ask any nurse in any specialty—ER, ICU, pediatrics, oncology—and you'll hear the same kinds of stories, just with slightly different props. Car accidents, sudden deaths, codes called overhead, traumatic injuries, angry family members, scared patients—nursing is *constant chaos*.

The only thing that saved me (and saved my patients from getting a version of me held together by coffee and panic) was a morning routine.

A morning routine is not some "cute wellness trend" when you're a nurse. It's armor. It's mental triage. It's your battle prep before stepping onto a unit where *literally anything* can and will happen.

Without a morning routine—some kind of grounding, reflection, or centering—you walk into that storm already behind. You become a reactionary nurse, a stressed-out nurse, a nurse who might survive their shift, but not come out truly on top. And if you stay reactionary long enough? You burn out. Fast.

A morning routine isn't about having more control over your day. It's about having more control over *yourself*—your energy, mindset, and patience—when the day inevitably spins out of control.

Because whether you're dodging sock missiles, decoding a patient's theology lesson, or simply trying to make it through 12 hours without mystery poop appearing somewhere on your body—you need something bigger than chaos to anchor you.

You need a system.

And it starts the minute you wake up.

Here's a guide to create a morning routine inspired by my practices and my mentor's (because I have to give credit where it is due), designed to foster mindfulness, gratitude, and focus. It has evolved for me, so please feel free to adapt and change it too! There is no right or wrong here because this is YOUR life you are creating!

Morning Routine Template

Most of it is done in the morning, so I call it my Morning Routine. It has three parts: The Routine, Affirmations, and Principles.

Read it every day, especially when you first start it, because this is your Vision Board. Add pictures and art to create something that you love looking at every day!

1. Morning Kickstart

    Time: 5-15 minutes

    Activity: Start daily with a warm cup of coffee or tea to awaken your senses. A smoothie containing greens, fiber, and vitamins will also do!

Purpose: Energizes the body and mind, preparing you for the day.

2. The 5 x 3 Routine

Total Time: 15 minutes

Activities:

Praying or meditating for others and expressing gratitude (3 minutes)

Gentle stretching or breathing exercises (3 minutes)

Reflecting on your goals and affirmations, and addressing any doubts (3 minutes)

Reviewing finances and investments (3 minutes)

Setting three main goals for the day (3 minutes)

Purpose: Focuses your intentions, aligns your spiritual and financial goals, and clarifies daily objectives.

3. Physical Activity

Frequency: Four times a week

Duration: One hour

Activities: Choose from walking, swimming, or using a treadmill.

Purpose: Enhances physical health and mental clarity.

4. Daily Social Media Engagement

Frequency: Once daily

Guidelines: Share insights on investing, rental tips, or personal wellness. Ensure the content is authentic and not forced. It can also be scheduled ahead of time so that you don't have to do it every day; it's just running in the background for you.

Purpose: Engage and grow your community while sharing valuable knowledge.

5. Partner Check-ins

Frequency: Three times per day

Activity: Connect with your spouse or a close friend to share positive updates.

Purpose: Maintains strong personal relationships and a positive outlook.

6. Self-Investment Time

Duration: One hour daily

Activities: Engage in educational activities, pampering, or learning a new skill.

Purpose: Promotes personal growth and self-care.

7. Daily Celebration

Duration: One hour

Activity: Engage in a loved activity to relax and enjoy, such as reading or taking a bath.

Purpose: Reinforces joy and satisfaction in daily life.

8. Evening Reflection

Activity: List three major wins of the day.

Purpose: Encourages a focus on success and positive outcomes.

9. Weekly and Monthly Reviews in the Morning
   Activities
   - Reflect on the most valuable activities.
   - Identify learning lessons and plan for upcoming challenges.

   Purpose: Provides a broader perspective on progress and future goals.

Affirmation Guide

Create affirmations that resonate with your personal goals and values. Here are some general tips to craft effective affirmations:

- Keep them positive and in the present tense.
- Ensure they are specific and relevant to your life.
- Repeat them during your morning routine to reinforce positive beliefs.

Example Affirmations:

- I work as little as I want and have everything I need to give to my loved ones with freedom and joy, not withholding. I give to others without limit.
- I am all I need to be today. I have everything I need right now. I am loved fully and share my abundance with everyone around me.
- All my bills are paid, and I have an abundance of money to share. Every time I pay a bill, I know I'm supporting someone with their daily needs. I am self-sufficient.
- I like my brain. It solves problems unexpectedly. Let it flow.

Remember, consistency is key to seeing the transformative impact of these practices in your life.

Principles to Live By

In addition to your morning routine and affirmations, integrating core principles or life philosophies can provide further guidance and inspiration throughout your day.

Below are principles, each accompanied by a motivational quote encapsulating its essence. These quotes can be from your favorite book, author, or even you! They can be reflected upon during your morning routine or throughout your day to keep you aligned with your values and goals.

1. Embracing Generosity

   Principle: Cultivate a spirit of generosity, giving more than expected in all interactions.

   Quote: Overpay everyone who works for you because "In the house of the righteous one there is abundant treasure" –Proverbs 15:6, NWT.

2. Pursuing Balance and Patience

   Principle: Balance action with patience, allowing natural progress without forcing outcomes.

   Quote: "Patience is a profitable virtue. Don't be greedy." –Kiana Danial

3. Focusing on the Positive

   Principle: Concentrate on positive aspects and solutions rather than dwelling on negatives.

Quote: "The law of polarity states that for every negative, there is a positive. You get the one you focus on." –Myron Golden

4. Cultivating Resilience

Principle: Build resilience by embracing challenges and using them as opportunities for growth.

Quote: "The only way to encourage change is to ruffle feathers. Kindly ruffle feathers." –Mandie Jo

5. Living Intentionally

Principle: Make intentional choices that align with your deepest values and desires.

Quote: "If it is meant to be, it will not end. The right plan or relationship will happen and will last. It is inevitable." –Brian Nox

6. Valuing Time and Decision-Making

o Principle: Value your time highly and make decisions quickly to harness the power of momentum.

o Quote: "Wealth is imaginary. Wealthy people make fast decisions." –Kiana Danial

7. Maintaining Mindfulness and Persistence

o Principle: Stay mindful and persistent, focusing on the present and appreciating what you will have with faith.

o Quote: "Keep on asking, and it will be given you; keep on seeking, and you will find; keep on knocking, and it will be opened to you" –Matthew 7:7, 8, NWT.

8. Embracing Spiritual Connectivity

   ○ Principle: Connect your actions to a higher purpose or spiritual path to enrich meaning in your life.

   ○ Quote: "There is nothing better for a man than to eat and drink and find enjoyment in his hard work. This too, I have realized, is from the hand of the true God" –Ecclesiastes 2:26, NWT.

9. Understanding Attachment

   ○ Principle: Embrace nonattachment to reduce suffering and increase peace. True peace and happiness come from letting go of these attachments and embracing a more detached, mindful approach to life.

   ○ Quote: "Attachment is the root of all suffering." –Buddha

Your vision and purpose may already be clear to you. Or maybe they are becoming clearer as we've touched the surface. Don't skip this step, whatever you do. It is not just a step but a routine that will carry you through the next phase of becoming a free nurse.

Check out my current Morning Routine and Vision Board on my website for more inspiration at *thefreenurses.com/my-personal-vision-board*

> **Affirmation #1:**
> I work as much or as little as I want. I have the financial freedom to design the life I live. I choose happiness today.

FREE NURSE ACTION CHECKLIST: START WITH VISION, NOT BALANCE

1. **Flip the Script.**
   - ☐ Let go of the myth of "work-life balance."
   - ☐ Ask yourself: What would my life look like if everything aligned with my purpose?

2. **Get Clear on Your Why.**
   - ☐ Write down your mission in one sentence.
   - ☐ Think: What fires me up every day? Who am I doing this for?

3. **Build Your Vision Board.**
   - ☐ Grab 5–10 images or quotes that inspire the life you want.
   - ☐ Post them where you'll see them daily (your phone, mirror, or notebook).

4. **Speak Life Over Your Goals.**
   - ☐ Choose 1–3 affirmations to repeat each morning.
   - ☐ Example: "I work as much or as little as I want. I choose freedom and joy today."

5. **Start Small, Stay Consistent.**
   - ☐ Choose one daily habit to support your vision (such as stretching, journaling, or reviewing your board).
   - ☐ Don't overthink it. Just start.

6. Celebrate the Wins.

☐ At the end of each week, ask yourself: What am I proud of? What aligned with my purpose?

☐ Write it down. Even tiny wins matter.

CHAPTER 2

THE POWER OF MENTORSHIP

Myth #2:
Hospitals and managers are the problem
(aka I hate my job, or if only "this" would change,
I would be happy).

Is Myth #2 heavy? You might read this and say, "I don't believe that! I love my job, I just don't like …" and then hear yourself rattle off the people, practices, policies, etc., that fill your day with angst and frustration. Or you might think, "Absolutely, they are the problem!"

Most nurses have felt it all, which might indicate that you are giving certain people and organizations way too much power over you. The healthcare system is broken in many ways— we all know that. Lots of things are broken in life, and that doesn't mean they should impact your happiness, right? We don't want to give hospitals or any organization or process that power. Thankfully, you and you alone are responsible for your happiness.

MEET JAMES: THE NURSE WHO COULDN'T BREATHE

James was the kind of nurse everyone wanted on their team.

Six-foot-two, former Army medic turned psych nurse, sharp under pressure, and a master at de-escalation. He could calm down a manic patient, train a new grad, and fix the wonky vitals machine all before his morning coffee.

From the outside, he looked solid.

But inside, James was suffocating.

He had two kids in elementary school, a wife trying to hold things together at home, and a mortgage that was eating him alive. He picked up OT every chance he got—partly to pay the bills, partly because *he didn't know how not to hustle.*

He told himself he was doing it for the kids. For the team. For the mission.

But he hadn't gone fishing in two years. He hadn't had a date night in eight months. On more than one occasion, he pulled into the hospital parking lot, sat in his truck, and wondered if this was all life had to offer.

One day, in a staff meeting, a colleague mentioned *"nurse burn-out"* like it was a buzzword. James wanted to laugh. Or scream.

He didn't feel *burned out*—he felt *boxed in.*

Then one night, at 2 a.m., James was doomscrolling TikTok on break when he saw a post from a nurse investor talking about passive income and "nurses who retire while still help-ing others."

That was the spark.

The next morning, James started building a vision board. He didn't tell anyone—not yet. He added a picture of a lake. A cabin. His wife laughing. A balance sheet with a line that said "dividends." And he started learning.

He opened a Roth IRA. Took an online course. Found a mentor who was already making money while working fewer shifts.

Today, James still shows up on the unit. But now he's got options. He turned a love for fitness into a part-time coaching biz. He teaches young guys in psych how to build strength—mental and physical. He has become a mentor in more ways than one.

He's still that rock for others, but now he's also built a foundation for himself.

He's not surviving anymore. He's designing.

He's not a stuck nurse. He's a *free* nurse.

WHAT'S BUGGING YOU IS GUIDING YOU

If mentioning your hospital, manager, team, or unit triggers negative feelings, this is the chapter for you.

However, triggers are a fantastic way of understanding what you value and what's most important to you. They are a window into your psyche and your soul. These are the problems at work that bother you the most and keep you up at night.

If it's bothering you, your body resists issues you don't seem to get past. Be thankful for your triggers. They are real and super important. Write down the triggers that relate to your job. We'll come back to them later once you have identified them.

_____

_____

_____

THE ROLE OF MENTORSHIP

Mentorship is one of the most effective tools at your disposal when navigating the complexities of nursing and the broader healthcare environment. A mentor offers guidance, emotional support, and wisdom. They can help you navigate the system, improve your professional skills, and find satisfaction and resilience in your career.

One of my first mentors in nursing school was Sharon Androes. She was my psychiatric-mental health clinical instructor and saw that I had a knack for mental health nursing. I would not be in the mental health field without her gentle encouragement, guidance, and passion.

Some of my first clinical nurse mentors were nurses in my unit who taught me everything they knew, generously sharing their hard-earned knowledge: Mary Hinkle, Ann Chowning, and Jenifer Mitchell. I'm mentioning names because we don't give enough credit to these nurses who shape and mold the next generation.

I've also had multiple leadership mentors: Melinda Waller, Caleb Jordt, Katie Dill, and Leslie Nyman. By the way, Leslie is not a nurse but thinks like a nurse and guards the good ones with motherly protection! She is an administrator whom I admire tremendously, and she has taught me so much about myself. I can always ask her for an honest opinion and kind but blunt direction.

That brings up a good point. Your mentors do not have to be nurses! They can be doctors, therapists, life coaches, or financial gurus. They often come into your life unexpectedly, just when you need them.

However, if you find yourself lacking one, here are some tips. If you are anything like me, and the thought of having a mentor freaks you out because it will feel like you have an accountability buddy looking over your shoulder, have no fear! Start slow and consider this chapter your first nurse mentor of sorts.

FINDING THE RIGHT MENTOR

Here's how to find a mentor who can help guide you through the nuances of your nursing career:

1. **Define Your Needs and Goals:** Clearly define what you hope to achieve before seeking a mentor. Are you looking for career advancement, skill development, or perhaps guidance on handling workplace dynamics?

2. **Look Within Your Network:** Start by looking within your existing professional network. This might include senior colleagues at your current hospital, former professors, or connections from professional nursing associations.

3. **Utilize Professional Associations:** Many nursing and healthcare associations offer formal mentoring programs. Joining these programs can connect you with seasoned professionals keen on guiding the next generation.

4. **Attend Industry Conferences:** Conferences and seminars are excellent places to meet potential mentors. They provide a natural setting for learning and networking.

5. **Consider Online Platforms:** Utilize professional networking sites like LinkedIn to find mentors outside your immediate environment. Many experienced professionals are open to connecting and sharing their knowledge virtually.

6. **Ask Thoughtful Questions:** Once you find a potential mentor, ask them thoughtful questions about their career path and experiences. This can help you determine if their expertise aligns with your needs.

7. **Formalize the Mentorship:** If someone agrees to be your mentor, discuss expectations for both parties. Determine how often you will meet and what goals you aim to accomplish together.

It's important to note that a mentor is not a friend. Not that you can't become friends, but ideally, mentors begin with an unbiased connection. They likely have not known you before, so they come in with a fresh perspective of you and are there to point out things that might be difficult to hear.

Remember, the goal of mentorship is to advance your career, enhance your personal growth, and ensure that your professional endeavors align with your values and aspirations. By actively engaging with a mentor and utilizing their insights, you can take meaningful steps toward becoming a free nurse.

Now, do you want real transformation? It's going to cost you something. For me, the price tag was $35,000—and it was the best money I've ever spent.

THAT'S WHEN I KNEW I HAD TO PAY

I was staring at the payment screen with sweaty palms. Thirty-five thousand dollars. That could cover a year of living expenses, a solid emergency fund, or a hundred things that felt more practical.

My fingers hovered over the keyboard. Everything in me was screaming: "Are you really going to do this?" And yet my nurse gut said yes.

For years, I believed mentorship should be free. If people truly cared, they'd just help. I figured I could patch it altogether with podcasts, books, and free advice. But then I heard my soon-to-be mentor say something that hit me right between the eyes:

"People who pay, pay attention."

She was right. That day, I realized I was either going to invest in myself now, or keep paying in delay, disappointment, and slow progress. And the truth is, I've never wanted to be a cheap person.

So, I did it. I made the payment.

And I showed up differently. No more playing small. No more being cheap. Because being cheap isn't just a money mindset—it's a statement about how you see yourself. Was I worth $35,000? Heck yes, I was.

That decision sparked a whole series of upgrades in my life.

I chucked the glitchy, low-budget internet that slowed down my business.

I hired a house cleaner (my mother, who then got to ditch her difficult clients and retire!) so I could spend more time creating and less time scrubbing.

I ordered fresh, healthy meals so I had more energy and fewer excuses.

I got my nails done and booked regular facials—not out of vanity, but because every one of those decisions whispered: I'm worth it.

And the results? They didn't just add up—they compounded. That investment gave me the education, confidence, and financial momentum I had been craving for years.

Paying for mentorship wasn't about the money. It was about the moment I stopped waiting to be rescued and finally bet on myself.

Think about all the free things you've gotten in life. Did you appreciate them as much as what you've worked hard for and paid for? Probably not. We take little things for granted every day, things that keep us alive, like oxygen and water. But something you've earned through time or money creates accountability, ownership, and a little pain for the sacrifice you made to get it.

Paying a mentor accelerates your growth. When it's intentional and both parties are aware of the goals and purpose, growth is exponential. For example, I wanted to learn about investing. I was 41, had no prior knowledge, and time was ticking.

When I discovered Invest Diva, it was everything I had ever hoped for. I found a group of like-minded individuals on the same path to financial freedom. I had already purchased the

PowerCourse, a self-driven course that teaches all things investing, and I made back five times what I paid for the course. To be transparent, I paid $2k for the course, and in just one year, I had made a profit of $10k.

So when I discovered that they offered mentorship and coaching for high-level professionals, my brain did the simple math. Okay, $35k could be 5x and become $175k ...?

As of the writing of this book two years later, I have made a profit of at least $85k. My portfolio, which was solely a 401k worth $119k, is now well-diversified with crypto and private equity assets, universal life insurance, an individual portfolio, and an IRA pushing $500k, all actively managed by me. So, I have not been disappointed. This is despite the market corrections and recession fears.

Paying for a mentor offers the accountability you might need, especially if you feel stuck in your role and life direction or have lost your mission and purpose. What's one area of your life where you've been playing cheap instead of choosing growth?

TRUSTING OTHERS

It might be hard to trust others, though, for various reasons. Brian Cerezo, The Money Nurse, sheds light on the challenges nurses face when it comes to trusting others, particularly in financial management and investing.

He attributes this hesitance primarily to the nursing profession's inherent need for control and precision. Nurses are accustomed to direct, hands-on management of their work environments, making it difficult to delegate or rely on others for advice.

Instead, nurses are expected to be the authority and have all the answers. "We are like absolute control freaks," Brian explains, noting how this trait, essential for patient care, complicates financial trust and support.

This need for control is further compounded by a lack of financial literacy within the profession, which Brian acknowledges is not sufficiently addressed during nurses' training or by healthcare institutions.

"The financial literacy is not there, and it's not our fault because it's just not taught," he adds, highlighting how this lack of education makes it harder for nurses to trust and utilize financial advice effectively. This combination of a need for control and a gap in financial education creates a significant barrier.

Brian Cerezo's journey from a New York City commuter nurse to a nurse millionaire vividly illustrates entrepreneurial grit and financial acumen. His initial investment forays were driven by a desire to escape the daily grind: "I work in New York City, I live outside the city, and the commute of an hour going to the city just started killing me the first year. And I was like, how do I get out of hating this commute, or how do I get out of this rat race?" This discomfort spurred him to explore investing to build a new life.

Brian's initial attempts at investing were rough and costly, marked by a steep learning curve: "I was young and naive and trying to look for that get-rich-quick thing. So I started with penny stocks, and I lost money quickly because I had no idea what I was doing."

However, these early setbacks did not deter him. Instead, they served as valuable lessons that redirected him toward more stable investments like dividend stocks, options trading, and eventually, real estate and cryptocurrency.

His strategic diversification paid off, particularly during the economic shifts brought on by the COVID-19 pandemic, leading to significant appreciation in his real estate investments: "Without the stock trading, I wouldn't have had the initial capital to get my primary house. Then, with the crypto trading, I did really well, which got me even more money to go into rental properties."

Brian's entrepreneurial mindset was further galvanized by personal life changes: "Once my kids came, I was like, now I have two kids' mouths to feed, and I need to make sure they're safe and protected." This realization pushed him to diversify his income sources further, integrating real estate and social media into his investment portfolio.

Brian's narrative underscores the transformation possible when nurses embrace an entrepreneurial spirit, trusting others and learning from their mistakes. So, what can you do?

Brian Cerezo offers practical advice on how nurses can move forward and get help with financial literacy and investment.

He advises, "I would say, go check out my course, but there are people like you, people like me that are putting out content that is going to show people what you need to do if you want to break out of nursing."

He encourages nurses to learn from those who have successfully navigated financial education, highlighting the role of mentors in guiding them through the complexities of finance and investment using trusted content and courses specifically tailored to their needs.

QUESTIONS TO PROPEL YOU FORWARD

If there is something still holding you back from taking the next steps to get a mentor, that's okay! To help you move past your current professional hurdles and take the next step, I will share some important questions you can ask to get yourself over the hump:

- What practical steps can I take to mitigate the triggers at my workplace?
- How can I contribute to positive changes within my work environment?
- What skills should I develop to better manage or avoid these challenges?

Write the answers here:

_____

_____

_____

_____

_____

_____

After asking yourself these questions, write down in two columns what you can control RIGHT NOW and what you can't. Start now:

I can control:	I can't control:

If you already have a mentor or are now considering getting one, bring the answers to these questions to them along with your list of triggers, what you can control, and what you can't.

Also, share your purpose, mission, and affirmations. It will get you started in a better place to become a free nurse. And that's what it's all about, right?

IS NURSING FOR ME?

After working on your affirmations, vision, and purpose, and engaging in the exercises outlined in the previous chapters and discussing them with a mentor, you might find yourself at a crossroads, questioning if nursing is truly the right profession. This realization can be both daunting and liberating.

It's important to remember that career paths are often non-linear and filled with varied experiences, including shifts and changes in one's professional life. Many nurses have transitioned away from direct patient care and the bedside. They have successfully channeled their skills and passions into other ventures like teaching, mentoring, real estate, writing, or digital marketing.

Some have transitioned completely from nursing, while others proudly wear their nurse badge, actively applying their nursing skills in various capacities. If you're contemplating a change, it's crucial to approach this decision thoughtfully. Here are three pivotal questions to ask yourself to determine if continuing in nursing is the right decision:

1. Do I feel energized or drained by my work days?
    o Assess how you feel at the end of most workdays. All jobs can be tiring, but feeling constantly drained

and dreading work can signify that nursing may no longer be fulfilling to you.

_____

_____

_____

2. What aspects of my job am I passionate about, and can these be fulfilled in another capacity?

   ○ Identify the parts of your job that bring you joy and satisfaction. Consider if these elements are unique to nursing or if they could be transferred to another field or role. This reflection can help pinpoint if your passion lies in patient care or the broader spectrum of healthcare and helping others.

_____

_____

_____

3. Am I staying in nursing because I feel it's expected of me or because I truly love it?

   ○ Reflect on the reasons you choose to stay in nursing. If external expectations (from family, society, or financial commitments) are the primary drivers rather than a genuine passion for the work, it might be time to consider a change.

_____

_____

_____

In addition, being a registered nurse comes with a ton of benefits. They are likely the reason you became a nurse in the first place. Here are the top 10. Ask yourself if these benefits are still important to you. Circle or highlight the ones that are, and write down the other reasons that are personal to you:

1. **Job Security:** The U.S. Bureau of Labor Statistics (BLS) projects that employment for registered nurses will grow by 6% from 2023 to 2033. This growth rate is faster than the average for all occupations. The BLS also estimates approximately 194,500 job openings for registered nurses each year over this decade, primarily due to the need to replace workers who transfer to different occupations or retire.[6] This growth reflects the high demand for healthcare services, especially as the population ages.

2. **Flexibility:** Many nurses benefit from nontraditional schedules. For example, 12-hour shifts that allow four days off each week are common in hospitals, providing flexibility for personal commitments.

3. **Diverse Opportunities:** According to the American Nurses Association, more than 100 nursing specialties allow nurses to work in fields ranging from forensic nursing to informatics. Each opportunity has its unique focus and setting.

4. **Competitive Salaries:** According to the U.S. Bureau of Labor Statistics (BLS), as of May 2023, the median

---

[6] "Registered Nurses," U.S. Bureau of Labor Statistics, August 29, 2024, https://www.bls.gov/ooh/healthcare/registered-nurses.htm.

annual wage for registered nurses was $86,070. The earning potential is significantly higher for specialized nursing roles, such as nurse anesthetists.

5. **Personal Fulfillment:** A study from the *PLOS One* journal found that nurses frequently cite making a difference in people's lives as a key source of job satisfaction, highlighting the personal fulfillment that comes from caring for others.

6. **Professional Development:** Nurses have pathways to advance their education through programs like RN-to-BSN or nurse practitioner degrees. For instance, the American Association of Colleges of Nursing notes a significant increase in nurses pursuing doctoral degrees, reflecting growth in professional development.

7. **Respect in the Community:** A Gallup poll consistently rates nursing as the most honest and ethical profession, a testament to the public's high regard for nurses.

8. **Ability to Make a Difference:** Nurses are often patients' primary caregivers. Their interventions have been shown to reduce mortality rates and improve outcomes. For example, a study published in *BMJ Quality & Safety* found that hospitals with a higher proportion of professional nurses experienced significantly lower mortality rates and higher patient satisfaction. Specifically, each 10% increase in the proportion of professional nurses was associated with an 11% decrease in the odds of patient deaths after general surgery.[7]

---

[7] Linda H Aiken et al., "Nursing Skill Mix in European Hospitals: Cross-Sectional Study of the Association with Mortality, Patient Ratings, and Quality of Care," BMJ Quality & Safety, July 1, 2017, https://qualitysafety.bmj.com/content/26/7/559?utm.

9. **Team Collaboration:** Nurses typically work in mul-
tidisciplinary teams that might include doctors, phar-
macists, and therapists. This collaborative environment
enhances patient care and creates dynamic work conditions that many nurses find professionally enriching.

10. **Global Mobility:** The World Health Organization
acknowledges the global mobility of nurses, highlighting
opportunities for them to work internationally. This not
only helps alleviate global health worker shortages but also
enriches nurses' professional and personal experiences.

IS IT JOB DISSATISFACTION OR DEPRESSION?

It is possible that you could be experiencing symptoms of
depression if you find yourself burned out, fatigued, and living each day with dread and sadness despite making efforts to
improve your mindset and situation.

Nursing, especially bedside nursing, is hard, but studies have
shown that the rewards of nursing typically outweigh the challenges and act as a protective mechanism from being burned out.

Determining whether feelings of unhappiness are due to job
dissatisfaction or a deeper mental health issue like depression
can be particularly challenging for nurses, who face high stress
and emotional demands in their roles.

Studies indicate that up to 18% of nurses suffer from depression, which is approximately twice the rate of the general
population.[8] Moreover, the accessibility of medications can

[8] Author Affiliations: Associate Professor of Nursing (Dr Letvak) and Statistician (Mr McCoy), "Depression in Hospital-Employed Nurses : Clinical Nurse Specialist," LWW, accessed April 12, 2025, https://doi.org/10.1097/NUR.0b013e3182503ef0.

lead to higher instances of substance abuse among nurses compared to other professions, with some reports suggesting that as many as 10-15% might struggle with drug addiction at some point in their careers.[9]

Alarmingly, a study from the University of California, San Diego, revealed that the suicide rate among nurses is significantly higher than the national average, highlighting the severe impact of mental health struggles in this field.[10]

If you or someone you know is struggling with suicidal thoughts or mental health distress, you can call or text **988** to reach the **Suicide & Crisis Lifeline**. This free, confidential support is available 24/7 to anyone in the United States.

If you are a nurse struggling to determine if your feelings are due to job dissatisfaction or depression, it's essential to look at the duration and extent of these feelings.

Depression is characterized by persistent sadness, loss of interest in enjoyable activities, and a range of physical symptoms such as changes in appetite and sleep patterns.

While it can lead to stress and unhappiness, job dissatisfaction typically does not encompass these broader psychological and physical symptoms. Depression symptoms are more pervasive and persistent, lasting more than two weeks, and can significantly impair one's ability to function, which differentiates them from general dissatisfaction at work.

---

[9] Addressing chemically dependent colleagues, accessed April 13, 2025, https://www.ncsbn.org/public-files/Addressing_Chemically_Dependent.pdf.

[10] J.E. Davidson et al., (2018). "Testing a strategy to identify incidence of nurse suicide in the United States." *Journal of Nursing Administration*, 48(5), 259–265.

PHQ-9 Depression Assessment

The **Patient Health Questionnaire-9 (PHQ-9)** is a widely used self-administered tool designed to assess the presence and severity of depression. It was developed in 1999 by Drs. Robert L. Spitzer, Janet B.W. Williams, Kurt Kroenke, and colleagues, with support from Pfizer Inc.

The PHQ-9 consists of nine questions that correspond to the diagnostic criteria for major depressive disorder outlined in the DSM-IV, making it a valuable instrument in both clinical practice and research settings.

The validity of the PHQ-9 was established in a seminal study published in the *Journal of General Internal Medicine* in 2001. This study demonstrated that the PHQ-9 is a reliable and efficient measure for diagnosing and assessing the severity of depression.[11]

This depression assessment may help you determine if you are suffering from depression. You might be familiar with it as it's frequently used in hospitals and clinics for our patients!

Please read each statement and circle the answer that best describes how often you have been bothered by the following over the past two weeks:

1. Little interest or pleasure in doing things

   ○   0 (Not at all)

   ○   1 (Several days)

---

[11] The PHQ-9, K. Kroenke, 2001, *Journal of General Internal Medicine.* Wiley online library, accessed April 13, 2025, https://onlinelibrary.wiley.com/doi/full/10.1046/j.1525-1497.2001.016009606.x.

   ○ 2 (More than half the days)

   ○ 3 (Nearly every day)

2. Feeling down, depressed, or hopeless

   ○ 0 (Not at all)

   ○ 1 (Several days)

   ○ 2 (More than half the days)

   ○ 3 (Nearly every day)

3. Trouble falling or staying asleep or sleeping too much

   ○ 0 (Not at all)

   ○ 1 (Several days)

   ○ 2 (More than half the days)

   ○ 3 (Nearly every day)

4. Feeling tired or having little energy

   ○ 0 (Not at all)

   ○ 1 (Several days)

   ○ 2 (More than half the days)

   ○ 3 (Nearly every day)

5. Poor appetite or overeating

   ○ 0 (Not at all)

   ○ 1 (Several days)

   ○ 2 (More than half the days)

   ○ 3 (Nearly every day)

6. Feeling bad about yourself, or that you are a failure or have let yourself or your family down

   ○ 0 (Not at all)

○ 1 (Several days)

○ 2 (More than half the days)

○ 3 (Nearly every day)

7. Trouble concentrating on things, such as reading the newspaper or watching television

○ 0 (Not at all)

○ 1 (Several days)

○ 2 (More than half the days)

○ 3 (Nearly every day)

8. Moving or speaking so slowly that other people have noticed. Or the opposite—being so fidgety or restless that you have been moving around a lot more than usual

○ 0 (Not at all)

○ 1 (Several days)

○ 2 (More than half the days)

○ 3 (Nearly every day)

9. Thoughts that you would be better off dead or of hurting yourself

○ 0 (Not at all)

○ 1 (Several days)

○ 2 (More than half the days)

○ 3 (Nearly every day)

Scoring: Total the scores for each item to get the final score. The higher the score, the more severe the depression. Here's how scores are generally interpreted:

- 0-4: None to minimal depression
- 5-9: Mild depression
- 10-14: Moderate depression
- 15-19: Moderately severe depression
- 20-27: Severe depression

Note: This tool is for screening purposes only and not for diagnostic conclusions. If you are experiencing any of these symptoms or have a high score, please seek professional medical advice.

If you rate for depression on this scale, you are not alone, and support is available. Resources such as the American Psychiatric Nurses Association offer directories to find therapists who specialize in helping healthcare professionals.

Additionally, many employers provide employee assistance programs (EAPs) that offer confidential consultations and therapy sessions. Online platforms like Talkspace or BetterHelp provide flexible options for receiving therapy at your convenience.

Woven throughout this book are insights from Judy Hu, LMHC, turned Boundary Coach. She has an amazing website, course, and coaching options that have helped nurses and healthcare professionals transform their relationship with their work. Please check her out, as well as other resources, because you are not alone!

Addressing mental health openly is vital, not only for your well-being but also for maintaining your ability to care for others effectively. Remember, seeking help is a sign of strength, and taking steps to manage your mental health is a crucial aspect of self-care.

It is recommended that all professionals have therapy regularly. A therapist is a form of mentor, and if it helps to think of one that way, do! Many healthcare professionals hesitate to see a therapist because of the stigma it can carry, so approaching it as a mentorship might reframe the situation. Paying for therapy will lead to those two benefits above: accountability and accelerated growth.

Professional Quality of Life Scale (ProQOL)

In the demanding field of nursing, distinguishing between clinical depression and the effects of job-related stress, such as burnout and secondary traumatic stress, can be challenging.

An invaluable tool in this process is the Professional Quality of Life Scale (ProQOL). Widely recognized and utilized by professionals routinely exposed to the suffering and trauma of others, the ProQOL helps measure both compassion satisfaction and compassion fatigue. The latter includes components like burnout and secondary traumatic stress, which can significantly impact your emotional and psychological well-being.

ProQOL is thoughtfully crafted to provide insights over 30 days, reflecting the positive and negative outcomes of professional caregiving. This self-assessment tool is especially beneficial for nurses who may experience high stress levels and emotional exhaustion. It offers a structured way to evaluate personal feelings and professional fulfillment, aiding in identifying if symptoms align more closely with job dissatisfaction or deeper emotional issues.

This scale is available for use through the generosity of the Center for Victims of Torture. For more detailed information and to access ProQOL, please visit ProQOL.org.

Remember, while this tool is helpful for self-reflection, it does not provide a clinical diagnosis. If your assessment results indicate significant burnout or secondary traumatic stress, consider seeking professional guidance or consultation to address these issues comprehensively. Often, though, this isn't burnout—it's misalignment. Let's fix that.

BOUNDARIES

No book for nurses would be complete without talking about boundaries for a moment. In a heartfelt discussion, I enjoyed exploring the crucial topic of boundaries in healthcare with Judy Hu, the boundary coach mentioned above, who has a rich background in mental health counseling and is one of the mentors I highly recommend.

Judy transitioned to boundary coaching to help professionals like us—nurses—understand and recalibrate our personal and professional limits. She describes boundary coaching as a means to "remind each person that I'm working with that their circle size is the same as everyone else's," emphasizing the importance of recognizing our worth and space just as much as we recognize others.

Judy shares a compelling visualization technique involving felt circles that she uses to teach the concept of boundaries. This approach simplifies complex feelings and visually demonstrates the need for expanding our boundaries.

She says, "It helps me concretize what's happening. It's a visual representation of, like, okay, so you need to expand your size, and what are you wanting?" This method resonates deeply, especially in a profession where we often feel overshadowed or smaller than others, particularly in high-stress environments.

During our conversation, Judy highlighted a challenge nurses and healthcare professionals face—the often ingrained cultural and gender expectations that dictate how we perceive and enforce our boundaries.

She reflected on her experiences, noting how she learned to believe that her "circle size was much smaller than others" due to her cultural background and professional environment. This insight is crucial for us, as nurses, who may similarly find ourselves shrinking in our professional roles, trying to fit into the molds prescribed by societal and cultural norms.

Judy's insights powerfully remind us to reassess and assert our boundaries, recognizing that we are not just caregivers but professionals who deserve the same respect, compensation, and consideration as our counterparts in all healthcare and professional fields. This reevaluation is vital not just for our well-being but also for the integrity of the care we provide.

As we continue to navigate our roles, Judy's wisdom offers both a mirror and a map, guiding us toward a healthier, more balanced professional life where our needs and contributions are fully acknowledged and valued.

In our conversation, Judy also delved into the psychological underpinnings that compel nurses and healthcare professionals to often put others before themselves.

This pattern is deeply ingrained in our training and professional culture. She explains how healthcare roles, especially nursing, are imbued with an expectation of self-sacrifice, which is celebrated but also often taken for granted.

The emotional and professional toll of these expectations during the pandemic was especially great, a time when the boundaries of personal risk and professional duty blurred dangerously.

Systemic changes are needed within healthcare institutions to better support nurses by recognizing their full humanity and professional worth. A reevaluation of compensation and work conditions that align more closely with the risks and responsibilities nurses undertake is needed.

"It doesn't really honor how much they're actually risking for the larger good," Judy remarked, capturing the sentiment that while society relies heavily on nurses, it often fails to appreciate them fully. Knowing this may also help you decide when to take a higher-paying position because you can set the boundaries of your wages and what you are worth.

WHEN IT'S TIME TO LEAVE YOUR POSITION

You may have reaffirmed your reasons for being a nurse through these first two chapters and are more committed than ever to your career choice. If so, congratulations! The next few chapters might surprise you about how to stay fully present in your purpose.

But first, there are some incredibly dysfunctional teams, hospitals, and organizations out there, and if you find yourself in one of them, staying may not be the best decision for you. Problems are designed, and we are not always aligned with a team's purpose, mission, and values.

Sometimes, the best solution is to leave your position and look for what better aligns with your purpose. This can be hard because we are endurers. We stick through thick and thin, sometimes to the detriment of our body and mind.

Unfortunately, nurses and healthcare workers can be exploited, mismanaged, and micromanaged. You aren't expected to endure abusive work environments.

Unhealthy environments, after all, will not help patients heal. Unless your passion is to rebuild these systems and you have clear boundaries about how much you will put up with, then leaving your position is necessary.

Fortunately, your daily positive affirmations will push you away from these negative work environments. Conversely, if you have a negative view of yourself, you may draw more toxicity to yourself because you lack the confidence to leave a difficult situation.

Be assured, you are worth so much more than that! This book will help you build that confidence. The rest of the book enables you to rely on your abilities to build the life you want rather than expecting a broken system to give it to you. Staying in a place where you don't have value or meaning and where you don't matter will never get you to a place of freedom and living your best nurse life.

A CURATED LIST OF 15 ONLINE NURSE MENTORS TO GET YOU STARTED

Here are some nurse mentors and coaches to consider. Most of these can be followed on social media, and you can learn and be inspired without paying a penny right now. Here are their Instagram handles and websites:

1. **April Rose (@nursemoneydate)**—Retired RN and finance coach, April focuses on teaching financial literacy and investment strategies to nurses. Website: Nursemoneydate.com

2. **Jumer Adalin (@jumeradalin)**—Helps nurses build profitable online presences, specializing in digital marketing and personal branding for healthcare professionals.

3. **Stacey Stegenga, RN (@investforfreedom_rn)**—Real estate investor and educator dedicated to teaching nurses about real estate investment opportunities. Check out her content for practical investment advice.

4. **Ellaina Maala, NP (@nursewhoinvests)**—Nurse investor and finance educator, Ellaina offers insights into the stock market and wealth-building strategies tailored for nursing professionals.

5. **Savannah Arroyo, RN, MSN (@networthnurse)**—Empowers nurses to take control of their finances through real estate investing and comprehensive net worth management. She shares practical strategies to build wealth, gain financial freedom, and create options beyond the bedside.
   Website: TheNetworthNurse.com

6. **Jayson Evangelista, RN (@jaysonevangelista)—** A dynamic nurse entrepreneur who inspires nurses to take control of their time, mindset, and financial future through innovative coaching and community-building.

7. **Tammy Lewis, RN (@nursebosssummit)—** Founder of Nurse Boss Summit, Tammy is on a mission to elevate nurses into empowered leadership and entrepreneurship roles. Her summit brings together top nurse leaders focused on business, branding, and impact.

8. **Jason & Monica (@nursestoriches)**—This duo focuses on showing nurses pathways to earning $200k+/year through diversified income strategies and advanced nursing roles.

9. **Brian Cerezo, RN-BC (@brianbenjiern)**—A podcast host and investor who shares insights into the financial markets and investment opportunities for healthcare professionals. Built an options course, Cash Care Plan, to teach nurses how to trade options as a side hustle. Website: www.stan.store/freenurses

10. **Angel Mathis, MN, MPH, ARNP, RN, FNP-Bc (@nurseinvestingforwealth and** www.freenurses. co/nifw)—Angel created the Nurses Investing For Wealth Method™, a monthly one-hour system that helps mid-career nurses manage cash flow, pay off debt, save, and invest with confidence—no financial jargon, no guesswork.

11. **Amy Burnie (@amyrburnie)**—A retired RN who focuses on helping nurses develop leadership skills and unshakable confidence in their professional roles.

12. **Nurse Meg RN (@nursemegrn)**—Specializes in tutoring and training for new nurses, offering guidance and education to ease their transition into clinical practice.

13. **Nurses on a Mission to Financial Freedom (@investingrnpod)**—A group dedicated to sharing stories and tips on achieving financial freedom through smart investing and passive income streams.

14. **Joshua Condado, CRNA (@thelifestylecnrna)**—A mentor and investor who combines his expertise in healthcare with financial savvy to guide other CRNAs.

15. **Imani Franks, BS, CPT (@thegoodgrowthg)**—Focuses on physical wellness and financial health, helping nurses and NPs achieve their fitness goals while managing their finances effectively.

FOUR MORE MENTORS YOU NEED TO KNOW

I had the privilege of interviewing two of the above nurse mentors, Brian Cerezo and Savannah Arroyo, as well as the following individuals who have inspired me beyond measure. Their wisdom and insights are sprinkled throughout this book, and I'm so grateful for their precious time.

1. **Kiana Danial** (@investdiva)—Kiana is a *New York Times* Best Selling Author and CEO of Invest Diva, which teaches students in over 130 countries how to be long-term investors. She has beaten the Wall Street bros at their game and made investing simple, fun, and incredibly profitable. Her Triple Compounding method

helped me build a $100k portfolio and earn $1k/month in dividends in less than 18 months. Learn more at www.freenurses.co/tcs.

2. **Judy Hu** is an LMHC turned boundary coach based in Massachusetts with almost two decades of clinical experience. Judy utilizes traditional talk therapy, mindfulness, guided visualization, somatic experiencing, and other trauma-informed interventions.

   Her book *The Boundary Revolution* is truly a revolution. It explores trauma in a whole new context. You must read it to understand how your culture and upbringing shape your boundaries. You can learn more on her websites, JudyHuBoundaryCoach.com and TheBoundaryRevolution.com.

3. **Preston Anderson** is a seasoned certified public accountant (CPA) who specializes in tax strategies for entrepreneurs. Preston is CFO, Owner, and Founder of Anderson Tax at andersontax.com and co-owner at Lolly's Home Kitchen with his wife.

   Preston's expertise is especially beneficial for nurses looking to navigate the complexities of tax planning to enhance their financial well-being. What I learned from him helped me get $37k back on my taxes in 2023, which I was over the moon about!

4. **Catarina Costa Abreu**, a healthcare economist and entrepreneur, is a powerhouse in healthcare economics and entrepreneurship, especially renowned for her dedication to empowering women in business.

With an impressive background that blends healthcare economics with a passionate, entrepreneurial spirit, Catarina is beyond talented and dedicated to helping women in STEM (science, technology, engineering, and math), particularly those of immigrant backgrounds, break free from corporate confines to pursue their entrepreneurial dreams. Her insight and guidance are pivotal for navigating the complexities of starting and scaling a business in today's competitive market.

Catarina's unique approach combines rigorous economic analysis with a deep understanding of the entrepreneurial landscape, making her an indispensable mentor for aspiring business owners. You can find her on TikTok and Instagram @adasiainsights.

THE MOMENT I ALMOST SUED THE HOSPITAL

After I was assaulted by a patient—hit in the face seven times, left with a concussion and bruises up and down my arms—I was furious, not just at the patient, but at the system.

Furious that I had let myself be left alone in a room with someone that unstable.

Furious that there wasn't better protection.

Furious that being per diem meant I didn't qualify for the hospital's extended illness coverage.

Yes, I got work comp, but the pay was measly and almost insulting. It felt like a second assault—this time on my skill, value, and years of experience. I didn't blame my unit or even my hospital specifically. But I wanted someone to be held accountable. I wanted someone to pay.

So, I did what many nurses dream about in moments like this: I looked into suing the hospital.

The attorney I met with came highly recommended by my therapist. And I'll be honest—I expected him to fuel my fire.

But what I got instead was a surprising dose of wisdom. We spent an hour discussing my life, future, and even the property I had just bought in Puerto Rico.

He listened. Then he said gently, "You don't want to sue the hospital. You're not going to get anything from it. Just keep focusing on you." He wanted me to focus on healing and living, not fighting.

I know attorneys get a bad rap, but I've been blessed with some of the best. The one who handled my divorce understood domestic violence inside and out. He supported me in ways I'm still grateful for today.

In fact, I found him through the Employee Assistance Program at the same hospital I'd once wanted to sue. That hospital also paid for my therapy after the assault.

That's when the emotional layers started to surface. The assault didn't just hurt because of the incident—it cracked open years of unresolved trauma. I had been in a domestic violence relationship for seven years. I had devoted myself to a religious system that kept me in that cycle, convincing me that endurance was the righteous thing to do. And here I was again—caught in another system that, on the surface, had failed me.

I felt stuck. Alone. Like I had no control.

So I threw myself a pity party. For two full weeks, I lay on the couch. I cried. I questioned everything. I rejected the sympathy cards, the calls, and the texts. I didn't want to talk to anyone.

And then, quite quickly, I started putting the pieces together. I was tired of being afraid and confused, so it didn't take long.

With the help of my friends, my family, my incredible nursing team, and eventually, the financial education and mindset work I discovered through Invest Diva, I started to understand the deeper truth:

Nurses stay stuck in situations that don't nurture them because they don't have a roadmap out.

They don't have mentors with their best interests at heart.

They stay in cycles of power and control, not realizing how much power they already hold.

The assault woke me up, not just to my pain, but to my purpose. I could keep blaming the system. Or I could build something stronger.

That moment, when I stood at the crossroads between vengeance and vision, taught me one of the most powerful lessons of my career: your healing is more important than your hurt. It's okay to be angry. It's okay to want justice. But staying there too long will steal your power.

What I discovered in the weeks and months after that assault wasn't just how strong I was, but how supported I had been all along. My nursing team, physicians, and leaders helped me escape my abusive marriage. It was messy, imperfect, and didn't look how I wanted it to, but there was support.

Sometimes, we miss it because we're too busy pointing fingers. That's when I knew: if I was going to heal, I had to start moving forward. Not alone, but with more mentors, therapy, financial education, and a new commitment to never outsourcing my power again.

You don't need to be rescued—you just need a roadmap. A mentor is that roadmap. And the journey? It's yours to begin.

Affirmation #2:
I fill my workplace with joy and happiness. I give and receive with open arms. I have unfailing support and resources at my workplace, and I am valued by my leaders and managers. My happiness is under my control, and I am happiness itself.

FREE NURSE ACTION CHECKLIST: RECLAIM YOUR POWER THROUGH MENTORSHIP

1. Check Your Triggers.

☐ Write down 1–3 things at work that consistently frustrate or upset you.

☐ Ask yourself: What do these triggers say about what I truly value?

2. Take Radical Ownership.

☐ Circle the triggers you can control.

☐ Cross out the ones you can't.

☐ Choose one action you can take this week to shift your mindset or environment.

3. Find a Mentor.

☐ Identify one person you admire professionally (nurse or not!).

☐ Reach out to a mentor with a simple question or ask to connect over coffee.

☐ Remember: mentorship doesn't have to be formal— just intentional.

4. Invest in Yourself.

☐ Ask: Where am I being cheap with myself?

☐ Choose one area to upgrade—your time, your tools, your therapy, or your self-care.

☐ Affirm: I am worth the investment.

5. Check Your Mental Health.

☐ Take the PHQ-9 or ProQOL assessment.

☐ Be honest about how you're doing.

☐ If your score is high, don't wait—reach out for support today.

6. Reclaim Your Boundaries.

☐ Reflect: Where am I shrinking to make others comfortable?

☐ Practice saying "no" with kindness and clarity.

☐ Remind yourself: My circle is just as big as theirs.

7. Ask the Big Question.

- ☐ Do I love nursing—or do I feel trapped by it?
- ☐ Journal your answer without judgment.
- ☐ Remember: You're not stuck. You're powerful. And you have options.

CHAPTER 3

FINANCIAL STABILITY THROUGH HOME OWNERSHIP

Myth #3:
Renting is better than buying a house
(aka I can't afford to buy a home).

I grew up poor in the 1980s. I lived in a trailer with my loving parents and brother. I was 15 when they bought our first house. Mind you, they had always owned their home. In fact, they never rented once in my youth. They owned the asset they lived in. Each time, save for the 2008 recession, their lifestyle and home improved as they moved. Why was that?

Because of something called appreciation. Homes appreciate in value due to several factors, including market dynamics, physical improvements, and economic conditions.

Location plays a critical role; homes in areas with robust economic growth or proximity to essential services like schools and transportation typically appreciate faster. For example, real estate markets near tech hubs like Silicon Valley have seen property values skyrocket due to high demand and limited supply.

Home prices have shown significant appreciation in my home state of Montana over recent years. From October 2019 to October 2022, home prices in Montana increased by 61%, substantially higher than the national average increase of 35.8% during the same period.

As of October 2022, the typical home value in Montana was approximately $467,068, reflecting an 18% increase from the previous year.[12] This robust growth in home values highlights Montana's increasingly attractive real estate market, driven by scenic beauty, a growing economy, and a desirable lifestyle that attracts residents and investors.

Economic conditions such as interest rates and inflation influence home prices. Historically, periods of low interest rates have correlated with increased home-buying activity, pushing prices up.

For instance, during the pandemic-driven low interest rates of 2020 and 2021, the U.S. median home price rose by over 20%, according to the National Association of Realtors.

Investments in local infrastructure can also boost home values. Studies have shown that new public transportation lines can increase nearby home values by up to 10%, with greater effects in highly congested urban areas.

---

[12] "Housing Market & Prices Montana 2023—Home Value Estimator," RealAdvisor, February 15, 2023, https://realadvisor.com/housing-market-montana/.

Furthermore, inflation tends to drive up home prices. Over the past 50 years, U.S. housing prices have risen at an annual average of around 4%, often aligning closely with broader inflationary trends. Buying a home is one way to meet or beat inflation. If you have money sitting in a bank, it will lose dollar for dollar every year.

The U.S. has targeted an inflation rate of around 2% as part of its monetary policy. However, post-2020, following the economic impact of the COVID-19 pandemic and subsequent fiscal and monetary policies, inflation rates have risen. For instance, in 2021, the inflation rate surged to about 7%, the highest since the early 1980s.[13]

So, let's say you bought a house in 2019 before the pandemic. Because you are a free nurse and you are thinking ahead (wink, wink), you bought a house worth $250,000; post-COVID, it is now worth 20% more, or $300,000.

Let's break down the calculation so you can see what I'm talking about:

- Initial Value: $250,000
- Increased Value: $300,000
- Appreciation: $300,000 / $250,000 = 1.20 (or 20% increase)

If we consider a rough estimate of inflation from 2019 to 2021:

---

[13] "Inflation (PCE)," Board of Governors of the Federal Reserve System, accessed April 12, 2025, https://www.federalreserve.gov/economy-at-a-glance-inflation-pce.htm.

- Inflation in 2019 was around 1.8%.[14]
- Inflation in 2020 was about 1.2% (impacted by the COVID-19 economic slowdown).[15]
- Inflation in 2021 surged to approximately 7% (*a sharp increase due to supply chain issues, stimulus spending, and economic reopening*).[16]

Using a compound interest formula to approximate the total inflation over these years would give a more accurate reflection than simply adding or subtracting inflation rates.

For each year, the factor would be compounded:

$$\$250,000 \times (1.018) \times (1.012) \times (1.07) \approx \$275,583$$

Thus, the house's increase to $300,000 indeed beats the compounded inflation rate increase, which suggests that the house's appreciation outpaced inflation.

Most people aren't crazy about math, but this calculation demonstrates that real estate investment substantially outperformed the inflation rate when considering the compounded effect.

You might say, "But I'm paying interest on a mortgage, so I'm not making as much." However, one of the key concepts of being a free nurse is learning what your government rewards. In

---

[14] "Consumer Price Index News Release," U.S. Bureau of Labor Statistics, January 14, 2020, https://www.bls.gov/news.release/archives/cpi_01142020.htm.

[15] "Consumer Price Index News Release," U.S. Bureau of Labor Statistics, January 19, 2021, https://www.bls.gov/news.release/archives/cpi_01132021.htm.

[16] "Consumer Price Index News Release—2021 M12 Results," U.S. Bureau of Labor Statistics, January 12, 2022, https://www.bls.gov/news.release/archives/cpi_01122022.htm.

this book, references are made to the U.S. government. The U.S. government rewards:

- Having children
- Owning a business
- Owning a home
- Owning long-term assets like property and stocks
- Going to college
- Being in the military
- This list goes on—it's all in the tax code

That's right. The tax code is not about taxes. Here, I diverge from home ownership specifically, just for a moment, to talk about taxes because they are all connected.

THE TAX CODE IS NOT ABOUT TAXES

The tax laws benefit anything that makes the government wealthier and protects its interests. The government is a business after all! (Hopefully, some CBT is happening right now, and your belief system will be challenged or confirmed. Remember CBT from Chapter 1?)

The tax code is a system of rewards, nothing more, nothing less. The government isn't out to get your money specifically. The tax code was built by the wealthy to support the wealthy and to keep the wealthy wealthy.

The forefathers of the U.S. government were very, very wealthy. It all goes back to where we learned this stuff, eh? Now, I doubt you want to have children or go to college just because the U.S.

government wants you to, but it's nice to know the benefits you are entitled to if you also want those things.

The U.S. government is not alone. Many countries that need citizens incentivize expats to leave their home country and live in theirs while enjoying premium benefits. So, you are in high demand, more than you know! Countries across the globe will pay you via tax incentives, credits, and deductions so you can bring your money and business to them!

Back to buying a home: homeownership significantly benefits the U.S. government by stimulating economic activity through increased consumer spending and job creation in the construction and home improvement sectors. It enhances fiscal revenues via property taxes and transaction-related fees, which fund local services and infrastructure.

Socially, homeowners tend to invest in their communities, contributing to stability and reduced crime rates. Politically, homeowners are often more engaged and provide stable voting patterns, aiding in the implementation of long-term policies.

Additionally, homeownership encourages wealth accumulation and reduces mobility, leading to workforce stability and reduced dependency on government assistance. These factors underscore why the government actively promotes homeownership through various incentives and policies.

What are some of the tax incentives you can get from the government for owning a home? As of the writing of this book, homeowners can deduct interest paid on up to $750,000 of mortgage debt from their taxable income, which reduces their tax liability. This means you are getting back the interest from the government while letting your property increase in value without taxation.

But what about the actual cost of borrowing money? Aren't you losing money there? Well, it depends. When you borrow money for less than it costs you, you are winning.

Does money cost money? Yes! Even your money costs money, especially when you don't invest and put it under your mattress. Borrowing money can often be financially advantageous compared to using your own money, particularly when borrowing costs are low and the potential return on investment (ROI) of the borrowed funds is high.

Here's a detailed example to illustrate why:

Example: Investing in Real Estate

Situation: You are considering purchasing an investment property that costs $300,000. You have $300,000 in savings, which you could use to buy the property outright, or you could get a mortgage and use some of your savings for other investments.

Option 1: Using Your Money

- You use $300,000 of your savings to buy the property outright.
- There's no debt, so no interest payments.
- The property appreciates at an average of 4% per year.
- Annual appreciation: $300,000 x 4% = $12,000.

Option 2: Borrowing Money

- You take out a mortgage for $240,000 (80% of the property price) at a 3% interest rate and use $60,000 of your own money as a down payment.

- Annual interest cost: $240,000 x 3% = $7,200.

- You invest the remaining $240,000 of your savings in the stock market, which historically yields an annual return of about 8%.

- Annual return from stock investment: $240,000 x 8% = $19,200.

- Property appreciation is the same at $12,000 annually.

- Net gain from property (appreciation - interest): $12,000 - $7,200 = $4,800.

Financial Comparison:

- By using your own money, your total gain is the property appreciation of $12,000 annually.

- By borrowing money, your total gain combines the net property gain and stock market returns: $4,800 + $19,200 = $24,000 annually.

By borrowing money at a lower interest rate and investing your funds in a higher-yielding asset, you leverage the use of borrowed funds to generate a higher overall return.

In this example, using borrowed money not only allows you to keep and potentially grow your liquid assets but also increases your total annual financial gains significantly compared to using your savings alone.

This scenario demonstrates the principle of "using other people's money" to increase potential returns while maintaining personal liquidity and diversifying investments.

This strategy is particularly effective in low-interest-rate environments and when there are higher-return investment opportunities. However, let's be more realistic about a high-interest-rate market.

Example: Investing in Real Estate with Higher Interest Rates

Situation: You are considering purchasing an investment property that costs $300,000, which you have in savings.

Option 1: Using Your Money

- You use $300,000 of your savings to buy the property outright.
- There's no debt, so no interest payments.
- The property appreciates at an average of 4% per year.
- Annual appreciation: $300,000 x 4% = $12,000.

Option 2: Borrowing Money at 6% Interest

- You take out a mortgage for $240,000 (80% of the property price) at a 6% interest rate and use $60,000 of your own money as a down payment.
- Annual interest cost: $240,000 x 6% = $14,400.
- You invest the remaining $240,000 of your savings in the stock market, which historically yields about an 8% return annually.

- Annual return from stock investment: $240,000 x 8% = $19,200.

- Property appreciation is the same at $12,000 annually.

- Net gain from property (appreciation - interest): $12,000 - $14,400 = -$2,400 (a loss due to high-interest costs).

Financial Comparison:

- Using your money, your total gain is the property appreciation of $12,000 annually.

- Borrowing money, your total financial outcome combines the net property loss and stock market returns: -$2,400 + $19,200 = $16,800 annually.

Even with a higher interest rate of 6%, borrowing money still provides a higher total return compared to using your savings alone. However, the margin of benefit is reduced significantly:

- The property incurs a net yearly loss due to the high-interest costs exceeding the appreciation.

- The overall financial gain is primarily driven by the stock market returns.

These trends demonstrate the significant impact of inflation on the value of money over short and long periods. It's important for economic planning and personal finance management to consider the eroding effects of inflation on the value of the dollar. You may realize there is no reason to wait or save for a house. You will start benefiting from the tax breaks right away! Your money will work for you while you sleep in your new house.

But is renting just as good as buying? Well, if your rent is $300/ month and you live with your family, then yes! That's a great deal. However, it doesn't mean buying property isn't a good deal. It's even better because you could rent your property as an investment and have someone else make your payment, all while building your wealthy nurse empire and paying $300/ month in rent.

But buying still makes sense for those who don't get cheap rent like that. To understand how renting compares with buying in the context of the previous example, we need to factor in rental costs, potential savings from not buying, and how those savings could be invested. Let's explore this scenario with specific assumptions:

Situation:

- Property cost: $300,000
- Interest rate: 6%
- Rental alternative: Renting a similar property for $1,200 per month ($14,400 annually)

Option 1: Buying with a Mortgage

- Down payment: $60,000
- Mortgage amount: $240,000
- Annual mortgage interest cost (not including principal): $14,400
- Property tax and maintenance: Assuming 1.5% of property value annually = $4,500

- Total annual cost of owning: Mortgage interest + property tax + maintenance = $14,400 + $4,500 = $18,900
- Annual property appreciation: 4% of $300,000 = $12,000
- Net cost of owning after appreciation: $18,900 - $12,000 = $6,900

Option 2: Renting

- Annual rent: $14,400
- Investment of savings: Investing the $60,000 down payment plus the difference in annual costs between owning and renting:
  - Annual savings from renting: $18,900 (owning) - $14,400 (renting) = $4,500
  - Total investable funds: $60,000 + ($4,500 annual savings, invested each year)
  - Assuming an 8% return on the total investable funds:
    - Yearly return on initial $60,000: $4,800
    - Accumulated additional investment return: Calculating this requires compounding the annual savings at 8%, but for simplicity, let's estimate the first year's return at 8% of $4,500 = $360

Financial Comparison:

- Buying: The net cost after appreciation and excluding equity buildup from principal payments is $6,900 annually.

- Renting: The cost of renting is $14,400, but with an investment return of $5,160 ($4,800 + $360), the effective net cost of renting is $14,400 - $5,160 = $9,240.

Analysis:

- In the first year, renting appears cheaper than buying when considering net costs after property appreciation, but not considering equity buildup in the home through mortgage payments.

- Over the long term, the calculation would need to account for the compounding of savings from renting, potential rent increases, and the equity buildup from paying down the mortgage principal.

- Other factors include changes in property value, potential tax deductions from mortgage interest (if applicable), and personal circumstances such as mobility needs and lifestyle preferences.

This is not financial advice. Buying or renting depends significantly on individual circumstances, market conditions, and long-term financial planning. In scenarios with high interest rates and moderate property appreciation, renting with strategic savings investment can sometimes offer a better financial outcome, especially in the short to medium term. However, buying can be advantageous for building equity and benefiting from potential long-term appreciation. And as free nurses, we are in it for the long term!

Let's say you want to move and no longer be in that house. It can still work to your advantage. You have two options:

- Turn it into an investment property. Rent it out and demonstrate income. Then, you will qualify for a new loan on your next primary home. Even more tax deductions that the government rewards!

- You can sell it, take the money you earned, reinvest in the next house, and use a Section 121 Exclusion if necessary.

The tax law allowing homeowners to sell their house and roll over the profits into a new home is the Section 121 Exclusion, or the Home Sale Exclusion. This law is part of the Internal Revenue Code and provides significant tax benefits to homeowners. Here's how it works:

Section 121 Exclusion (Home Sale Exclusion)

1. Primary residence exclusion:
   - Up to $250,000 of capital gains can be excluded from the sale of a primary residence for single homeowners and up to $500,000 for married couples filing jointly.
   - To qualify, the homeowner must have owned and lived in the home as their primary residence for at least two out of the last five years before the sale.

2. No requirement to roll over profits:
   - Unlike the old law (pre-1997), which required homeowners to roll over profits into a new home to defer capital gains taxes, the current Section 121 Exclusion does not require this.

○ Homeowners can use the excluded capital gains for any purpose and are not required to reinvest the profits into a new home.

3. Frequency of Use:

○ This exclusion can be used once every two years. If you sell your home and exclude the gain, you must wait at least two years before you can exclude the gain on another home sale.

Example:

● Single homeowner: If a single homeowner sells their home for a $300,000 profit, they can exclude $250,000 from capital gains taxes. They would only pay taxes on the remaining $50,000.

● Married homeowners: If a married couple sells their home for a $600,000 profit, they can exclude $500,000 from capital gains taxes. They would only pay taxes on the remaining $100,000.

Key Points to Remember:

● Primary residence: The property must be your primary residence, meaning you have lived in it for at least two out of the last five years.

● Exclusion limits: The exclusion is capped at $250,000 for single filers and $500,000 for joint filers.

● Frequency: The exclusion can be claimed once every two years.

- No rollover requirement: There is no requirement to roll over the profits into a new home to receive the tax benefit.

This provision significantly benefits homeowners. It allows them to exclude a large portion of their capital gains from taxation, providing substantial financial flexibility and reducing the overall tax burden associated with selling a primary residence. Homeowners can also deduct their property taxes.

Moreover, don't overlook the importance of shopping around for the best mortgage deals. While I've had mixed experiences with online lenders like Better.com, exploring various financing options is crucial. My interactions with multiple local banks and paying in cash have helped build strong banking relationships and facilitated smoother transactions.

One reason for this is that nurses have such a stable income, they are like the veins that pop out at you when you are about to draw blood. Banks can't wait to poke us! They know we have access to bonuses, our job is in high demand, and we have a reputation for being the most trusted profession.

A wealth of information is available about owning a home, but nothing compares to the actual experience. My number one tip for getting started is simple: just do it. Don't hesitate or wait until you feel ready—sometimes, diving in is the best way to learn.

Begin by shopping around for a real estate agent who fits your needs; remember, while compatibility with your agent is important, ultimately, it's about finding the right property.

Utilize tools like Zillow and Rocket to explore options easily. Personal referrals can also lead to reliable agents—our family, for example, has worked with the same local agent for over two decades.

However, remember that what works locally may not suit out-of-state transactions. I've also successfully bought properties remotely without ever meeting the agent or seeing the site.

THE ONE THAT GOT AWAY: MARCUS'S REGRET

Marcus had been a solid, steady presence in the ICU for nearly a decade. The kind of nurse who always picked up extra shifts, handled pressure like a pro, and trained new grads like a big brother.

He'd been renting the same two-bedroom apartment in Denver since 2014. It was close to the hospital and cheap—well, it *used* to be. His rent had nearly doubled, and every year his landlord reminded him, "Hey, at least I didn't raise it *more*."

Marcus had considered buying a place more than once. His credit was decent. He had a small down payment saved.

But every time he got close, he talked himself out of it. "What if I want to move?" "What if something breaks?" "I'm not ready for all that responsibility."

Then one day, in 2023, while scrolling through Zillow, he saw it: the exact townhouse his buddy Trevor had bought down the road for $240,000 in 2016.

It had just sold for $520,000.

Marcus's heart sank.

That could've been *his* equity. *His* house. *His* leverage to leave the bedside, take a travel gig, or buy back his time.

Instead, his rent was higher than Trevor's mortgage—and he had nothing to show for it.

That moment stuck with him.

He wasn't afraid of the mortgage anymore. He was afraid of missing out on the next chance to build wealth just because he kept waiting to feel "ready."

Why Home Ownership?

Why am I so staunch on home ownership, and why do I consider it one of the first steps to becoming a free nurse? The answer lies partly in my financial journey—transforming a $550,000 investment into properties now worth millions.

I'm not a CPA, and this book isn't a tax guide or financial advice (although I do have some advice from a CPA for you!). This is what I did to pave my way to a current asset worth of nearly $2 million and a net worth of $1.3 million and counting.

My Million Dollar Property

In 2017, my then-husband and I built a second home, investing approximately $550,000. This was in addition to our first home, the first property I had ever owned. This new home was my last-ditch effort to save my marriage. I had hoped that creating a home my husband loved might bring him happiness.

Deep down, I knew this wouldn't work, that his problems were much deeper than any material asset could solve. But I had to try, as I always strive to give my best in any situation.

After moving, rather than selling, we decided to rent out the original property we purchased in 2015. We divorced not long after building the new home in 2017.

Throughout our marriage, I had been the primary earner, which gave me the financial stability to secure loans. The new home only appraised for $462,000, short of our $550,000-plus investment, but because I knew the power of property ownership, I did not want to sell.

We lived in Northwest Montana, the home to beautiful Glacier National Park. Montana is dubbed the last best place for a reason, and I was sure the home's value would increase.

I obtained loans through my connections with banks and loan officers I knew. I bought both homes and even paid him half of my retirement because Montana is a 50/50 state!

It paid off. Unbeknownst to us, the rest of the world, and all the poor healthcare personnel, COVID would hit in 2020, which would soon double home prices in Montana.

THE DAY I REALIZED I WAS A MILLIONAIRE

It wasn't some big celebration. There was no champagne pop or camera-ready moment. I was in my pajamas, coffee in hand, sitting on the couch in the quiet stillness of an early morning. I had just pulled up Zillow—mostly out of curiosity.

I typed in my home address, the one I had poured so much of myself into. The one I had fought to keep after my divorce. The one I had refinanced, along with the divorce settlement I owed instead of selling because I *knew* deep down it had value that hadn't been realized yet.

When I saw the number on the screen, I blinked twice.

That can't be right.

I refreshed the page. I checked the comps. I even pulled up my loan documents and did the math by hand. And then I sat back slowly in my chair, heart pounding with a quiet, stunned gratitude.

I'm a millionaire.

It wasn't loud. It wasn't flashy. But in that moment, everything clicked. The sacrifices. The fear. The hard decisions. The courage to keep a house that hadn't appraised high enough. The late nights figuring out how to refinance and make it work if it was worth it. The therapy. The trust in my gut.

They all led here.

That house didn't just shelter me. It *set me and my family free.*

And I realized—there was nothing magical or elite about it. It wasn't luck. It was ownership. Literally and figuratively. I owned the property, yes—but more than that, I had started to own my decisions, my financial future, my freedom.

After selling that home, I made several strategic moves that significantly altered my financial landscape. I purchased condos in Puerto Rico and Oregon, which I now operate as short-term rentals, generating a steady stream of passive income.

Additionally, I acquired another condo that's easier to maintain and serves as my primary residence, which I might consider renting out in the future. My investments also extended to improving the lives of my loved ones: I bought cars for my parents, grandmother, and friend, and an RV for our family.

I've successfully retired my parents. I've also enjoyed sending my family and friends on vacations. Financially, I've placed our assets into family trusts, launched my business, and built a diverse stock portfolio. Two years after that pivotal sale, these decisions, rooted in home ownership and patience, have profoundly transformed my life.

My backstory might be unique, but the principles of wealth-building through real estate are universal. By buying property in Northwest Montana, an area known for its natural beauty and growing real estate market, unbeknownst to me, I capitalized on geographic desirability—an often overlooked aspect of real estate investments.

When the unexpected hit—like the market boost from COVID-19—my property's value soared, illustrating how market dynamics can favor well-positioned real estate investments.

Stories of Nurse Real Estate Investors

I'm just one of many examples of nurses who have propelled themselves to become real estate millionaires. I already introduced Brian Cerezo, The Money Nurse, and his journey from a novice investor to a property-savvy nurse with a substantial net worth.

His initial motivation sprang from the daily grind of commuting to New York City, which he quickly realized was unsustainable. "The commute ... just started killing me," Brian explained. This frustration sparked his interest in investing to escape the "rat race."

Despite initial setbacks in the risky realm of penny stocks, where he lost $5,000 to $10,000, Brian shifted toward more stable investments like dividend stocks and eventually real estate. This move stabilized his finances and set the stage for significant wealth accumulation.

His real estate journey began with acquiring his primary residence, funded by stock and cryptocurrency trading gains. Brian's real estate strategy focused on affordability and favorable landlord laws, leading him to purchase rental properties in Ohio—a decision driven by lower costs and more landlord-friendly regulations compared to New York.

He described the strategic choice: "I didn't want to property manage anything myself ... and living in New York, it's one of those states where the tenants have all the rights and the landlords have zero rights." This highlights the importance of geographical considerations in property investment, an essential tip for nurses looking to invest outside their home states.

A trusted property management team facilitates the management of these properties. "They are everything to me because all they do is send me a text every month with all the information on the rent and if there are any . . . calls or what needs to be done." Trust and delegation are key to managing distant investments effectively.

In her inspiring journey toward financial freedom, Savannah Arroyo, MSN, RN, also known as the "Networth Nurse," discovered the transformative potential of real estate. With a background in nursing and a master's degree in Nursing Leadership and Administration, Savannah has seamlessly transitioned her skills into real estate investment.

Her journey began with a desire to create a lifestyle prioritizing family time and financial independence. Once a healthcare professional grappling with the demands of a high-stress job, Savannah's life took a pivotal turn after the birth of her second daughter.

This milestone prompted her and her husband to reevaluate their lifestyle and financial strategies, leading them to explore multiple streams of income. Real estate kept appearing as a promising avenue during their research, drawing Savannah into its depths.

Once she delved into real estate investing, initially educating herself through podcasts and books, she quickly realized that it offered not just a path to wealth but also the autonomy she yearned for.

Savannah and her husband decided to focus primarily on real estate, which led them to discover the power of real estate syndications. These are ventures where individuals pool their resources to invest in properties that would be out of reach financially on an individual basis, like large apartment complexes or mobile home parks.

Savannah learned the ropes of syndication, mastering the art of value-added opportunities—investments where the property is enhanced to increase its income and worth. These projects could drastically uplift rental income by addressing undermarket rents and untapped property potential, thus significantly boosting the property's overall value.

Her success with syndications altered her financial landscape and reshaped her personal life, granting her the freedom and time she desired with her family.

Savannah's story is a testament to the power of real estate investing to achieve significant financial returns and personal liberation. It encapsulates a journey of learning, investment, and growth. Today, she empowers other healthcare professionals to explore passive income opportunities in real estate, helping them secure a prosperous future without sacrificing their passion for caregiving.

As you can see, Savannah and Brian's stories, along with mine, are not just about financial gain but also about achieving personal freedom and improving the quality of life for our families.

If these resonate with you, be assured you have what it takes to follow our blueprints. Financial and personal emancipation through real estate investment is possible, and it is one of the first investments you could make to get your feet wet if you haven't already.

LET'S TALK MILLIONAIRES

You've met several nurse millionaires in this book already, and it's important to understand the types of millionaires you will encounter as you build your wealthy nurse empire!

How wealth is accumulated and measured can categorize individuals into at least nine types of millionaires. You might find that you already qualify as one:

- **Net Worth Millionaires**: Individuals whose assets, minus liabilities, total at least $1 million.

- **Liquid Asset Millionaires**: Those who possess easily convertible assets such as cash and stocks, amounting to over a million dollars.

- **Income Millionaires**: People who earn an annual income of at least $1 million.

- **Real Estate Millionaires**: Owners of property valued at over a million dollars.

- **Investment Millionaires**: Those who have achieved this status through investments in stocks, bonds, and other securities.

- **Cash-Flow Millionaires**: Individuals who generate over a million dollars annually from their investments or businesses.

- **Business Valuation Millionaires**: Entrepreneurs who own a part of a company valued at over a million dollars.

- **Accredited Investor Millionaires**: Investors who meet specific net worth or income criteria that allow them to invest in higher-risk securities.

- **Retirement Millionaires**: People who have amassed over a million dollars in their retirement accounts.

Each category represents a different facet of financial success and avenues for wealth accumulation. Personally, I have achieved the status of a real estate millionaire and a net worth millionaire.

Additionally, I am actively working toward becoming a retirement, liquid asset, investment, and cash-flow millionaire. Isn't it exciting to know that nurses these days can easily become millionaires with the right strategy?

A CPA'S PERSPECTIVE

Preston Anderson is a seasoned Certified Public Accountant whose expertise in tax strategies for entrepreneurs is super down-to-earth and understandable. As the founder and CFO of Anderson Tax, Preston brings a wealth of knowledge and experience to the financial arena, helping business owners maximize their financial well-being.

His approach simplifies the often complex world of taxes and ensures his clients achieve the best possible outcomes for their personal and business finances. Here are five key recommendations from my interview with Preston Anderson that offer valuable insights for nurses and other professionals regarding tax strategies and real estate investments:

1. **Duration of home ownership**: He advises that buying a home generally makes financial sense if you plan to stay in it. "The rule of thumb is usually five years. If you're going to be in a home for over five years, it generally makes sense." This is due to the associated costs of buying and selling, which can offset property appreciation over time.

2. **Real estate as an inflation hedge**: Real estate is described as a solid hedge against inflation because it tends to appreciate at a rate that matches or exceeds the inflation rate, thus preserving the value of your investment. "Real estate is a wonderful, wonderful hedge against inflation."

3. **Leverage and risk in real estate**: He points out that leverage (using borrowed money to increase the potential return of an investment) can amplify both gains and losses. Understanding this can help manage risk when investing in property. "If it goes up 3%, you don't go up 3%, you go up 15%. But if it goes down 3%, you don't go down 3%, you go down 15%."

4. **Benefits of owning real estate long-term**: Long-term real estate ownership can lead to substantial profit through appreciation and leveraging tax benefits like depreciation and the possibility of a step-up in basis for heirs. "If you're going to be there or if you're going to hold the property for longer and turn it into a rental, buying real estate is phenomenal." Property can also be transferred easily to heirs via family trusts.

5. **The emotional and strategic impact of buying a home**: "Buying a home for me and my wife has been the best decision." He shared that they profited substantially from their first two homes, underscoring the financial opportunities that real estate can offer over time.

Ready or Not

Zach stared at the pre-approval letter sitting in his inbox. It wasn't huge—just enough for a modest starter home outside of town—but it was real.

He hovered over the "Reply" button. *I'm not ready,* he thought. *I should wait until I'm more settled. Maybe next year.*

A year later, that same neighborhood had jumped $70,000 in value. His rent? Up again. His regret? Even higher.

Zach didn't lose because he made a bad decision.

He lost because he didn't make one.

MY PERSPECTIVE: BUY YOUR FIRST HOUSE BEFORE WORRYING ABOUT WHETHER YOU CAN AFFORD IT

In wrapping up this chapter, it's clear that home ownership isn't just about securing a living space—it's about establishing a foundation for financial security and personal fulfillment.

As you've seen from my journey and countless others, real estate can transform your financial landscape, offering stability and opportunities for significant growth.

Whether you're a seasoned nurse or just starting out, remember that stepping into the real estate market is not merely a property investment but an investment in your future. The journey to becoming a free nurse is paved with the bricks of wise investments.

If you're ready to be a free nurse, the time to act is now—by exploring your real estate options and connecting with real estate experts who can guide your path forward.

Embrace the process, learn from each experience, and use the resources available to make informed decisions. And buy your first house before worrying about whether you can afford it. This is not financial advice, and I am not a CPA, but in the next chapter, you'll learn why buying your home now is so important. The reality is you can't afford not to.

> **Affirmation #3:**
> I can handle the responsibility of home ownership and the wealth it creates.

FREE NURSE ACTION CHECKLIST: BUILD WEALTH THROUGH HOMEOWNERSHIP

1. **Bust the Myth.**
   - ☐ Say it out loud: "Renting forever is not the only option."
   - ☐ Ask yourself: *What's the real reason I think I can't buy a home?*

2. **Check Your Mindset.**
   - ☐ Do I see homeownership as a burden or a stepping stone to wealth?
   - ☐ Affirm: "I can handle the responsibility of home ownership and the wealth it creates."

3. **Run the Numbers (Without the Fear).**
   - ☐ Look up what homes are selling for in your area—just start browsing.
   - ☐ Use a mortgage calculator (Rocket, Zillow, NerdWallet) to see what your payment *might* be.

4. **Start Your Team.**

☐ Ask a friend or coworker for a real estate agent referral.

☐ Talk to one lender—just to learn. You're not committing yet!

5. **Leverage What You Learn.**

☐ Learn what tax benefits you'd get just by owning a home.

☐ Think about future moves: rent it out, refinance, or sell and reinvest.

6. **Remember This Truth.**

☐ Homeownership isn't just a dream—it's a *strategy.*

☐ Buying your first house isn't about being "ready." It's about building wealth that works *while you sleep.*

CHAPTER 4

MANAGING FINANCES

Myth #4:
Nurses should be paid more
(or I need a higher degree to make more money).

In today's economic climate, where inflation is a persistent upward force and interest rates climb, everyone feels the pinch—nurses included. It's a common sentiment that wages should rise to match increasing living costs.

Compensation should keep pace, particularly for nurses, who are vital to our healthcare system. However, the economic reality paints a different picture. Due to structured wage scales and economic limits, nurses, like many others, find that their income growth is capped—they consistently earn more than CNAs but never approach doctors' salaries.

This might seem disheartening, but viewing it as a limitation places the burden of your financial prosperity on the healthcare system's ability and willingness to pay more. A free nurse does not give a hospital, spouse, government, or any other institution the power to achieve freedom.

To achieve financial freedom, relying solely on nursing wages is not sufficient. Believing that nurses should be paid more is a limiting belief. It is true! Nurses should be paid more, as should everyone working hard to save lives every day and caring for a community's health.

But believing it puts the onus on the hospital and healthcare system to fulfill your financial wishes. You will not become financially free solely by relying on nurse wages UNLESS you invest them and make your money work for you as hard as you do for your patients.

For nurses navigating the complex financial landscape of today's economy, mastering effective financial management techniques is crucial. This chapter offers practical advice and tools to help manage finances with an eye toward long-term stability.

Maya Angelou famously said, "If you don't know where you've come from, you don't know where you're going." You gotta know how much you are making to understand how much more you want to make to invest.

A CLEAR PATH TO TAKING CONTROL OF YOUR FINANCES

For almost seven years, I lived in a relationship that was terrifying, confusing, and completely isolating. It was emotionally, physically, and financially abusive—and I didn't see it clearly at first.

He convinced me it was my fault. That I caused it. That I deserved it. That no one would believe me. That I shouldn't tell anyone.

I've been called a b*tch more times than I can count. I've had objects thrown at me, been bruised, smothered, and threatened with harm, suicide, and murder.

I begged him to get rid of the gun under the bed. He refused. He would scream, manipulate, and then act completely normal—sweet, even—which was the most confusing part. Then he says I did the same thing, gaslighting me. I began to question my reality.

And financially? He drained me. The person who was supposed to provide for me took advantage of me, using personal resources that I didn't want to use.

I've since learned that I'm not alone—many nurses and healthcare workers experience financial abuse in their relationships, in their families, and in the very systems that employ them. Our compassion and expertise are a prime target for narcissists, criminals, and sociopaths.

The abuse didn't end when I left. He stalked me. Recorded me. Tried to reach me through family. It's like they want to keep a hold on your nervous system forever—just enough to keep you feeling unsafe, unseen, and small.

But here's what I know now: every act of financial empowerment is an act of resistance. Budgeting, investing, not making rash decisions and selling—those weren't just financial moves for me. They were *survival strategies*. And then they became *freedom strategies*.

If you're reading this and you've experienced any form of financial or emotional control, I see you. Escaping is scary and dangerous. And there is help:

National Domestic Violence Hotline ☎ 800-799-7233 | 📱 Text START to 88788 | 🌐 www.thehotline.org

Whatever situation you are facing: bankruptcy, debt, abuse, you don't need anyone else's permission to take your power back. Not your partner. Not your employer. Not your past.

Acknowledge the Reality of Your Financial Situation

The first step in managing finances is acknowledging the reality of your financial situation, which can be daunting. Many people like to just look the other way.

It can be scary to see the reality because it may give us a seemingly bleak outlook on our future. And nurses, well, we tend to expect a lot of ourselves. This is why I want you to buy your first house before you start managing your finances. Silly, you say? Here is why:

A bank won't loan to you if it thinks you are too risky. Banks require a lot of documentation to prove that you are a good investment for them. They verify your financial status, income, identity, and creditworthiness. They will ask for:

- Recent pay stubs (last 30 days usually) and possibly an employment verification letter
- W-2 forms from the past two years
- If self-employed, 1099 forms and/or profit and loss statements
- Federal tax returns (last two years)
- Additional income documentation (bonuses, alimony, royalties, etc.)
- Contact information for your employer(s)
- Permission for the lender to run a credit check (the lender will pull your credit report)

- Details of current debts (auto loans, student loans, other mortgages, credit cards, etc.)
- Personal and business bank statements from the past few months (usually two to six months)
- Statements for investments (stocks, bonds, retirement accounts) over the last few months
- Documentation of real estate or other assets owned
- Documentation showing the source of your down payment (e.g., savings account statement, gift letter if a relative is gifting the money, etc.)

If you are in your first home, you've already done half the work for this step, which means you are almost there. Digital tools can help you track every dollar and understand your spending habits. And this begins a series of Rich Tips ...

Rich Tip #1: Download Empower at www.empower.com and build your financial profile. It's free, and you can create budgets designed to help you understand your current financial situation, which you'll do in the next section.

If you feel anxious about your financial situation, affirm: "I am abundant. I have everything I need today."

MEET ERICA: THE NURSE WHO DIDN'T KNOW WHERE HER PAYCHECK WENT

Erica was a full-time nurse with a part-time Amazon habit. If burnout had a scent, hers smelled like espresso pods and Bath & Body Works candles. She made decent money—$45 an hour plus differentials—but somehow, every two weeks, her paycheck vanished like a patient before vitals.

She'd scroll TikTok between night shift admits and hit "Buy Now" faster than you could say "Doordash." "I deserve it," she'd whisper, tapping her card for overpriced oat milk lattes and cute but unnecessary nurse gear. Budgeting? That sounded like punishment.

Then one day, her Discover card got declined … *at Taco Bell.* Humiliated, she opened her banking app and nearly dropped her Crunchwrap. It wasn't just one bad month. It was every month.

That night, instead of doomscrolling, she downloaded Empower and connected all her accounts. Within 24 hours, she saw the truth: $1,172.88 on Amazon in the last 30 days. Over $300 on coffee. And hundreds more on recurring subscriptions she didn't even use.

She didn't delete Amazon, but she created an "Erica Treats" budget line and capped it at $200. She turned off one-click ordering. And she scheduled a weekly "money date" every Sunday, with candles and a good playlist.

Now she calls herself a "Budget Baddie" and has paid off two credit cards. Her latte habit? Still alive—but now it's earned with reward points.

Creating a Budget

Once you know where your money goes, you can create a budget that fits your financial needs and goals. Begin by clearly showing your income and where each dollar is spent.

As a nurse, you're likely to have a stable income; however, expenses can often creep up and be unaccounted for, and you might not realize what you are spending your money on! Here are the top 10 categories where nurses typically spend their money:

- **Housing:** Whether it's mortgage payments or rent, housing is usually the largest monthly expense for most nurses.

- **Transportation:** This includes car payments, fuel, maintenance, and possibly public transportation costs, especially commuting to work.

- **Healthcare:** Despite working in the industry, nurses still incur personal healthcare expenses such as health insurance premiums, co-pays, prescriptions, and possibly additional costs for family members.

- **Food and Groceries:** Daily living expenses cover food, including groceries for home-cooked meals and dining out.

- **Utilities and Home Maintenance:** Regular monthly expenses such as electricity, water, gas, internet, and phone bills, along with home maintenance and repair costs.

- **Education and Professional Development:** Many nurses invest in ongoing education and professional development, including tuition, textbooks, seminars, and workshops, to maintain licensure or advance their careers.

- **Childcare:** For nurses with families, childcare can be a significant expense, including daycare, babysitting, or after-school programs.

- **Retirement Savings:** Contributions to retirement accounts like 401(k)s, IRAs, or other pension plans are a priority for future financial security.

- **Leisure and Entertainment:** Spending on hobbies, vacations, movies, books, and other forms of entertainment that provide relaxation and personal enjoyment.

- **Clothing and Personal Care:** This includes not only general clothing but also specialized apparel, such as scrubs and footwear for work, along with personal care products and services.

Don't focus too much on how you can cut back. Instead, look for ways to create the life you want with what you earn today. Develop a mindset of abundance and wealth, and allocate funds to what truly makes you happy.

For example, I love to spend money on my family and help them have a more comfortable life. I choose to spend money on supporting my parents' retirement, family goals and careers, and luxuries like vacations. This means I choose to cut back on my expenses, like:

- **Transportation:** I own older vehicles, which are cheaper for insurance and taxes. Currently, I own a 2000 VW Jetta and a 2010 Honda Pilot. They each have over 200,000 miles on them! I don't have car payments and keep my cars well-maintained, so they don't break down frequently. I always own at least two vehicles at all times so that I'm not stranded when one needs maintenance. If one eventually dies, I won't be pressured to buy a new one right away. It's a sort of emergency fund for cars!

- **Healthcare:** I do the math to choose which insurance plan meets my needs to keep costs down. I have purchased both a traditional and a High Deductible Health Plan (HDHP). HDHPs have low premiums but higher upfront out-of-pocket costs. Employers often pair an HDHP with a Health Savings Account (HSA) to help you cover some or all of your deductible. Generally speaking, if you are healthy, you can pay less with an HDHP, save tax-free money in an HSA, and invest it in the stock market when you aren't using it.

HSAs and FSAs (flexible spending accounts) have tax limits, and it's best to contribute up to the limit, depending on which you choose. I typically do not choose dental or vision plans. I've done the math, and it's generally more expensive to have one unless you are getting some serious work done.

- **Food and Groceries:** One of the most significant expenses most people incur is food, specifically eating out. Boy, I love to cook and eat out lavishly, but I save this for vacations and special occasions now.

  I take advantage of the abundance of food in the U.S. and eat for free or at a low cost almost everywhere I go. It's amazing how easily you can manifest free food at work, your parents and grandparents, friends, and places you wouldn't even consider. Especially when working in hospital settings, wouldn't you agree that people are always bringing food to eat?

  I'm not suggesting taking advantage of people. The very people feeding me are often the people I'm working for or supporting and caring for monetarily. It's one way I've recognized how my generosity repays itself!

So look for similar things in your life. Next time your hospital throws you a pizza party, be thankful for it instead of complaining, and see how the mindset shift brings you even better meals next time.

I also have meals delivered, which saves time and money. And let's be honest, cutting back on how much you eat might even be good for your health *and* your wallet—because tightening your belt doesn't just have to be financial, it might also help your waistline.

- **Clothing and Personal Care:** With online shopping and delivery, everything can be automated now. This is really helpful with budgeting because you can set up deliveries based on what you actually need and plan ahead.

  I use Amazon, InstaCart, and Costco to find the best deals, set them, and forget them. I also find that I manifest things like furniture, clothing, and personal items easily, so include these in your affirmations. You might be surprised what shows up on your doorstep in your abundant mindset! Don't forget to be grateful and thank the universe so it keeps coming, and you can share what you are getting.

Budgeting is very personal, and it's important to have a budget you enjoy looking at every day. Does that sound silly? It's not! Have a budget that excites you and reminds you of your purpose and goals. Look at it every day for 90 days and keep tweaking it until it feels right for you.

Rich Tip #2: Set up your first budget in Empower and use its automatic categorization for all of your expenses. Make sure you connect all of your credit cards and bank accounts. You can also use Credit Karma or another budgeting app of your preference, but Empower offers the best overall options for starters. Some apps don't let you create budgets, so choose one that does.

Setting Up an Emergency Fund

An emergency fund is a financial safety net designed to cover unexpected expenses such as medical bills, car repairs, or sudden job loss. Typically, it's recommended to have a three-to-six-month buffer.

For nurses who have a sick leave benefit already, I recommend starting with a three-month safety net. It's an easier goal to achieve, and using a high-yield savings account can help you grow your savings faster than traditional savings accounts.

While the average savings rate in the U.S. hovers around 0.40%, many online banks and credit unions offer high-yield accounts with competitive rates, sometimes exceeding four or five times the national average.

It's important to note that this is not a savings account, and I'm not encouraging you to save. Avoid the mindset that you can become a financially free nurse by saving. You can't. Investing in property and the stock market can make much better returns. Investing in assets is where it's at, nurses!

Saving your money is a myth you were taught in school or by your parents. An emergency fund is different. These are liquid funds (aka easy to use) that you don't touch unless you absolutely need to, or only touch if you have an investment opportunity too good to pass up.

Either way, you don't want money sitting there making only pennies. It must work for you in a HYSA (high-yield savings account) while your other funds are invested in assets.

Rich Tip #3: Open a HYSA today and set up an automatic monthly transfer to build your emergency fund. Don't worry about how much you are putting in, just start saving today to get into the habit. It can be $25, $50, or $100. Just start so you can see the high interest start paying you back. Go to www.forbes.com/advisor/banking/savings/best-high-yield-savings-accounts/ to see all the options. Look for the current highest yield backed by the FDIC and with no fees.

STRATEGIES TO CAPITALIZE ON EASY INCOME AND REDUCE DEBT

There are some very easy ways to earn extra income that people miss out on every day. Wealthy people take advantage of these constantly, and you can too!

Credit Card Rewards: In 2014, an individual made headlines for amassing an astonishing 422 million credit card rewards points, showcasing the potential extremes of credit card rewards strategies.

This example is not an isolated incident; there are numerous stories of "credit card churners" who meticulously manage multiple credit cards to optimize reward points, miles, or cash back.

For instance, another enthusiast reportedly earned over a million miles by purchasing more than $3,000 worth of pudding during a promotion offering frequent flier miles. Points can be redeemed for luxury travel, first-class flights, upscale hotel stays, and even cash back, turning everyday purchases into profitable returns.

I made $3036.47 cash back in 2023 with my credit card reward programs, and that doesn't include my fly miles card redemptions and other upgrades or discounts I get for being a loyal customer.

Rich Tip #4: The Free Nurse Credit Card Playbook. Every nurse needs these three credit cards:

- **Citi Double Cash:** The best overall credit card for everyday expenses. It rewards you with cash back for spending and paying with your card for a total of 2%.

- **Chase Amazon:** If you love Amazon, you must get the Amazon Prime Chase card, which offers 5% back on every purchase. If you use Amazon's subscription service, you get 5-15% more on your purchases. It's such a screaming deal!

- **Costco Citi Card:** The best card for gasoline, travel, and restaurant rewards. Especially for Costco lovers!

For more of my favorite credit cards, go to thefreenurses.com/credit-cards-and-banking.

High-Interest Debt Reduction: The flipside of credit card rewards is making sure you pay them off every month. This is a must. Do not pay high interest on credit cards! Tackle high-interest debts head-on by first paying down the most costly debts. You can use Debt Payoff Planner to organize and prioritize your debts for repayment. Use it free on iOS or Android, or access the full web version at debtpayoffplanner.com.

If you want to do it without an app, it's also simple. Just pull out your credit card statements, car loan statements, personal loans, and any other debts you may owe. Look at the interest rates and start by paying off the one with the highest interest rate.

Don't worry about home mortgages, student debts, and home equity lines of credit (HELOCs). These all offer tax advantages and are generally examples of good debt! That's right, debt can be a good thing. It gives you access to assets that create more wealth for you. You want that kind of debt. However, credit card debt charging more than 8% is not in your best interest.

Rich Tip #5: Search for credit card balance transfer offers. Chase, Citi, Bank of America, and U.S. Bank are some credit cards I have used to transfer balances. Many offer around a 5% balance transfer fee.

Opening another credit card can increase your credit score by lowering your debt ratio, giving you more available credit. So it's a win-win. Commit to yourself that you will pay it off by automating your monthly payments, and then start using your other credit cards to earn rewards and pay them off monthly with auto-pay.

Retirement Savings Plans: I'm not a fan of 401(k)s for a few reasons. First, there can be hidden fees that the institution charges. Second, you usually can't manage your own money and choose what companies you invest in. Third, the institution can change the terms at any time.

For example, a few years back, my 401(k) through Vanguard quit paying me dividends. I'm still fuming about it. That said, taking full advantage of any employer-sponsored retirement plan is still profitable if it offers matching contributions. That's free tax-deferred savings that also grow tax-deferred. Don't contribute more than the match, though. You can make higher returns with an individual portfolio after learning the Invest Diva Diamond Analysis and applying the principles from the Triple Compounding System.

Rich Tip #6: Check with your HR department about matching contributions and ensure you maximize this benefit.

Rich Tip #7: **Begin your personal investing journey now** by taking the free Triple Compounding Masterclass. This method helped me reach a portfolio of **$407,952.12 in just two years**— all while working full-time as a nurse. You'll learn more about the Triple Compounding method in the next chapter, but **don't wait to take the first step.**

Start now. Every day you delay, you leave money on the table and time on the clock. Your future self will thank you. Join the masterclass by using this URL: www.freenurses.co/tcs.

TAX-ADVANTAGED SAVINGS—THREE THINGS EVERY NURSE SHOULD GET

1: Get an IRA

Investing in an individual retirement account (IRA) can significantly enhance long-term financial security. IRAs come in two main types—traditional and Roth—each offering specific tax advantages tailored to different financial scenarios.

A traditional IRA provides tax-deferred growth, meaning the contributions are potentially tax-deductible based on your income level and participation in employer-sponsored retirement plans.

Withdrawals during retirement are taxed at ordinary income rates, ranging from 10% to 37%, depending on your total retirement income. This type of IRA is beneficial if you anticipate being in a lower tax bracket during retirement than your current one.

On the other hand, a Roth IRA offers tax-free growth and withdrawals, suitable for those who expect to be in a higher tax bracket in the future. Contributions to a Roth IRA are made with after-tax dollars and aren't tax-deductible, but withdrawals are tax-free in retirement. There is an income phase-out range for contributing to a Roth IRA that changes annually, so you'll want to be aware of the current limits.

Additionally, setting up a Custodial IRA (either Roth or traditional) can be a strategic move for nurses with children who have earned income. An adult manages these accounts until the child reaches adulthood and operates under the child's social security number.

This early start on savings provides a financial head-start for children and introduces them to the principles of investing and saving, potentially leading to significant financial growth over time due to compounding interest.

When considering how much to invest each month into an IRA for themselves and a Custodial IRA for their child, nurses should assess their overall financial situation, including their current income, expenses, and financial goals. Here's a guide to help determine the appropriate amounts:

For the Nurse's Own IRA:

- **Maximum Contribution Limits**:

    Each year, the IRS sets a maximum amount individuals can contribute to a traditional or Roth IRA. These limits are subject to annual adjustments based on inflation. Individuals age 50 or older may qualify for an additional catch-up contribution, allowing them to contribute more than the standard limit to support their retirement savings goals.

- **Monthly Investment Strategy:**

  To maximize your IRA contributions, divide the annual limit by 12 to create a consistent monthly investment plan. This approach helps build the habit of saving while taking full advantage of your yearly tax-advantaged contribution limit. If you're eligible for catch-up contributions, adjust your monthly amount accordingly to meet the higher threshold.

These contributions are pre-tax for a traditional IRA, potentially lowering your taxable income. In the case of a Roth IRA, contributions are made with after-tax dollars but allow for tax-free growth and withdrawal, which can be particularly beneficial if you anticipate higher tax rates during retirement.

For the Child's Custodial IRA:

- **Earnings Requirement**

  To contribute to a Custodial IRA, a child must have earned income. This can come from part-time jobs, freelancing, or even helping out in a parent's business. If you're self-employed, hiring your child is a win-win— you can deduct the expense as a business cost and build long-term wealth for them through a tax-advantaged retirement account.

- **Contribution Limits**

  The annual contribution limit for a Custodial IRA is the same as that for an adult IRA. However, you can only contribute up to your child's total earned income for the year, whichever is less. So if they earn $3,000 in a year, that's the max you can contribute on their behalf. These limits are adjusted periodically for inflation by the IRS.

- **Monthly Investment Strategy**

  If your child earns money consistently, you can break their eligible contribution into manageable monthly amounts. For example, to contribute $3,000 over a year, you'd invest $250 per month. Consistent, automated contributions over time can turn small earnings into major growth thanks to the power of compound interest.[17]

Ideally, you want to max out both your IRA and your child's IRA. Assuming an annual average rate of return of 8% and a max contribution of $6,500 annually (these contribution limits could increase in the future, but hypothetically speaking), after 20 years, you would have approximately $297,456 in your IRA.

So if you feel you are starting late, perhaps you are in your 40s and feel a bit behind like I do, don't stress! If you took that same amount and put it in a regular savings account with low interest, you would only have about $130,000. Quite the difference, huh?

---

[17] "Roth IRA for Kids: PLAN Benefits, Eligibility, and Investment Options," Fidelity, accessed April 13, 2025, https://www.fidelity.com/retirement-ira/roth-ira-kids.

Let's say you have been saving for your child like this. After 60 years, your child would have approximately $2,355,437 in their IRA (assuming an annual rate of return of 8%). What a gift!

This example demonstrates the power of compounding interest over a long period. Compounding is when your investment returns earn you even more returns over time. Here's how it works: When you invest $500 and earn a 10% annual return, your balance grows by $50 to $550 after the first year.

Then, in the next year, assuming you get the same rate of return, your balance grows to $605, a $55 gain. Imagine that little extra oomph playing out over years or decades—that's how compounding can help you build a comfortable retirement nest egg, even with smaller contributions.

How much should you set aside each month to hit your IRA goal? Use this free online savings calculator to crunch the numbers based on the current limits: www.forbes.com/advisor/retirement/traditional-ira-calculator/

Rich Tip #8: Set up a Roth or traditional IRA today on Robinhood. Robinhood often offers a small match of funds for an extra boost. My affiliate link is https://join.robinhood.com/mandieh-f88067. This will also help you prepare to create your investment portfolio when we start that in Chapter 5.

2: Get an HSA or FSA

I mentioned how I save money by contributing to an HSA or an FSA. It's your turn to make this happen!

Health Savings Account (HSA)

An HSA is a tax-advantaged savings account for individuals enrolled in a high-deductible health plan (HDHP). Contributions are made pre-tax, lowering your taxable income, and funds grow tax-free and can be withdrawn tax-free for qualified medical expenses.

- You can contribute up to the annual limit set by the IRS, which is typically higher for those with family coverage versus individual coverage.
- Individuals age 55 or older can make an additional catch-up contribution each year to boost their savings.
- Unlike FSAs, HSA funds roll over year to year, and the account stays with you, even if you change jobs or insurance plans.

Flexible Spending Account (FSA)

- An FSA is another type of pre-tax account offered by many employers, designed to help you save money on healthcare or dependent care expenses.

There are two primary types:

- **Health FSA**: Can be used for eligible medical expenses like co-pays, prescriptions, and over-the-counter items.
- **Dependent Care FSA**: Covers qualifying child care expenses (e.g., daycare, after-school programs, summer camps).

Contributions to both types are **pre-tax**, lowering your overall taxable income.

These accounts offer pre-tax benefits, reducing your taxable income and providing a method to save for medical and dependent care expenses. FSAs generally have a use-it-or-lose-it rule, although plans may allow a carryover of up to $660 into the following year for health FSAs.

Both HSAs and FSAs offer tax advantages, such as pre-tax contributions, which can reduce your taxable income.

Rich Tip #9: Look at your health insurance. Do you qualify for an FSA or HSA? You will qualify for one or the other. Make sure you are contributing the maximum to get a full tax deduction. If you have an FSA and aren't using it every year, consider switching to a high-deductible health plan.

3: Get a 529 College Savings Plan

- Purpose: Specifically designed to save for future college expenses.

- Benefits: Earnings grow tax-free if used for qualified education expenses like tuition, books, and room and board. Some states also offer deductions or credits on contributions.

For parents, these accounts not only help in managing savings efficiently by earmarking funds for specific future needs but also offer various tax advantages that can significantly enhance financial growth over time. It's advisable to consult with a CPA to tailor the right mix of accounts to your family's specific financial goals and needs.

Individuals can set up a 529 College Savings Plan. This flexible feature allows adults to save for their higher education expenses, including tuition, mandatory fees, books, supplies, and certain room and board costs. This can be particularly useful for adults considering returning to school or pursuing further education later in life.

When you open a 529 plan, you can name anyone as the beneficiary, including yourself. The account owner retains control over the funds and can change the beneficiary at any time if they decide not to use the money for their educational expenses. This makes it a practical choice for lifelong learners or those planning a career change that requires additional qualifications.

Additionally, some states offer tax benefits, such as deductions or credits, for contributions to a 529 plan, which can further enhance the savings even when the plan funds the owner's education.

Rich Tip #10: If you want to further enhance your repertoire or save for college tuition for your children, a 529 plan is a must! Each state manages 529 plans differently. Go to www. nerdwallet.com/article/investing/529-plans-by-state to learn how to open one where you live.

Rich Tip #11: Schedule a weekly financial review as a recurring event on your calendar. For financial literacy, budgeting tools, and coaching, visit me and these other nurse colleagues to find your best fit.

- Mandie Jo, Free Nurse—www.thefreenurses.com
- Savannah Arroyo, Real Estate Coach— www.nethworthnurse.co
- Brian Cerezo, Options Coach— https://stan.store/freenurses
- Angel Mathis, Wealth Coach—www.freenurses.co/nifw

ELEVATING NURSE WAGES THROUGH SPECIALIZATION

Reflecting on the constraints of nursing salaries and the need to ensure your finances are as productive as you are, it's enlightening to consider the experiences of nurses who've significantly increased their income without getting a second degree. Many have pursued travel nursing, moved to higher-paying states, or specialized in lucrative niches.

Personally, I work at a hospital renowned for rewarding its staff with substantial incentives for additional shifts, preferring this approach over relying on travel nurses. My compensation has averaged $100 per hour, factoring in certification pay, preceptor pay, retention bonuses, shift differentials, and other variable incentives.

Typically, I could work about 60 hours weekly, taking time off when I want to rest up from my busy schedule. While this intense schedule isn't for everyone, nor is it my long-term plan, nor guaranteed, it does lend itself to a unique discovery for myself and others: Getting a higher degree is not the fastest way to achieve a higher income. It certainly can improve your credibility, help you get the schedule you want, and help you reach your aspiration goals, but it may not pay higher wages. Note these wages for bedside RNs compared to APRNs. Here are the top five highest-paid specialty bedside nurse positions as of the writing of this book:

1. **RN First Assists** are registered nurses who support surgeons directly during procedures, playing a vital role in the operating room. They typically earn an average annual salary of **$124,509**.

2. **Operating Room (OR) Scrub Nurses** help maintain a sterile environment during surgeries, prepare surgical instruments, and assist throughout the procedure. Their average annual salary is around **$124,509**.

3. **Intensive Care Unit (ICU) Nurses** provide short- and long-term care to patients with life-threatening conditions. They are trained in emergency response and critical care, with opportunities to specialize in adult, pediatric, or geriatric ICUs. The national average salary for ICU nurses is about **$118,199** per year.

4. **Cardiovascular Operating Room (CVOR) Nurses** are highly trained surgical nurses who assist in heart surgeries and related procedures. They typically earn an average annual salary of **$105,456**.

5. **Infection Control Nurses** specialize in preventing and managing the spread of infections within healthcare environments. They develop protocols, educate staff, and respond to outbreaks. Their average annual salary is around **$103,938**.

The average salary for an **Advanced Practice Registered Nurse (APRN)** in the United States was approximately **$129,480** as of May 2023, according to the U.S. Bureau of Labor Statistics. This figure includes nurse practitioners, nurse anesthetists, and nurse midwives. Compensation may vary depending on experience, specialty, and location.[18]

---

[18] "Home," U.S. Bureau of Labor Statistics, March 14, 2025, www.bls.gov/ooh/healthcare/nurse-anesthetists-nurse-midwives-and-nurse-practitioners.

1. **Certified Registered Nurse Anesthetists (CRNAs)** are consistently the highest-paid among APRNs, with an average annual salary of $214,200.[19]

2. **Psychiatric Nurse Practitioners**, though grouped within the broader nurse practitioner category by the BLS, typically earn salaries close to or slightly above the median, around **$135,000**, depending on their practice setting and region.[20]

3. **Neonatal Nurse Practitioners** have reported median salaries of about **$122,500**, with total compensation (including benefits and bonuses) averaging **$130,500**.[21]

4. **Hospitalist Nurse Practitioners**, who manage inpatient care and often work in collaboration with hospitalists and physicians, have average annual earnings ranging from **$95,000 to $140,000**, with a reported average of approximately **$113,883**.

5. **Pediatric Nurse Practitioners** earn an average annual salary of approximately **$125,924**, as noted in a 2021 salary guide from Barton Associates.[22]

These figures represent base salaries and can vary widely depending on geographic location, experience, and the specific

[19] Nurse anesthetist salary by state [2024] - nightingale, accessed April 14, 2025, https://nightingale.edu/blog/nurse-anesthetist-salary.html.

[20] Masters in nursing salary & highest paid jobs | USAHS, accessed April 14, 2025, https://www.usa.edu/blog/master-science-nursing-salary/.

[21] EveryNurse Staff, "Neonatal Nurse Practitioner: Salary & Jobs," EveryNurse.org, June 12, 2024, https://everynurse.org/careers/neonatal-nurse-practitioner.

[22] "Pediatric Nurse Practitioner Salary Guide," Nurse.org, accessed April 13, 2025, https://nurse.org/education/pediatric-nurse-practitioner-salary/.

health facility. However, you can see that advanced practice RNs don't make that much more than bedside RNs on average. And so many nurses are making even higher wages annually than above, without advanced degrees.

Rich Tip #12: Subscribe to Brian Cerezo's YouTube Channel and watch all the interviews of nurses making $200,000 to $500,000 annually, including my interview here! www.thefreenurses.com/options-cash-care-plan.

Notably, some nurses achieve similar earnings to mine without overtime by moving to states or hospitals that pay better. Keeping an open mind to all the options and being flexible in managing our work lives is crucial as we aim for both financial wellness and personal fulfillment.

A FINAL THOUGHT ON WAGES: STRATEGIC ADVOCACY BY NURSES FOR NURSES

Despite these opportunities for higher income, the broader issue of nurse valuation remains critical. In a revealing discussion with Catarina Costa Abreu, a seasoned healthcare economist, the complexities of healthcare economics and its direct impact on nurses were brought to light.

Catarina shares what health economists do: "We try to quantify the benefits and the costs, not just the financial but also the clinical costs, like health costs, the cost to quality of life," etc., underscoring the profound implications of economic decisions in healthcare, which then impact wages.

Catarina emphasizes nurses' often-overlooked yet pivotal role in wage valuation, advocating for their greater involvement in policy-making, which can also significantly influence healthcare practices.

"Nurses are often the unsung heroes in our healthcare narratives. They execute care plans, manage patient interactions, and bear the brunt of system inefficiencies while often remaining invisible in discussions about healthcare funding and policy decisions," she reflects. This stark portrayal highlights nurses' need to engage more actively in hospital boards and quality review panels, where they can wield considerable influence.

By grasping the nuances of healthcare economics, nurses can better advocate for their rights and those of their patients, ensuring a more judicious allocation of resources. "It's about understanding not just your role in providing care but also the broader economic impact of that care. This knowledge empowers nurses to participate in conversations that shape the healthcare landscape," Catarina concluded.

Engaging deeply in healthcare economics and policy-making improves nurses' working conditions and potential wages and also ensures that the healthcare system becomes more responsive to providers and patients.

This engagement fosters a more transparent, effective, and equitable healthcare environment, empowering nurses to leverage their unique positions and knowledge to effect meaningful changes within the system.

The complexities of healthcare economics might seem distant from the day-to-day tasks of nursing, yet they directly influence all aspects of healthcare delivery, including your wages. Engaging in policy-making and research allows nurses to ensure that their frontline experiences inform healthcare decisions, leading to more relevant and effective services.

Even at the unit level, nurses can get more involved in making changes that impact their work environment. By advocating for better wages and conditions, they can influence healthcare economics at a systemic level, enhancing both their working conditions and the quality of patient care.

CONCLUDING THOUGHTS

Managing resources effectively, having a budget that you like to look at routinely, embracing modern financial tools, and making choices about how you spend your money are crucial for nurses to achieve financial freedom. Understanding the economy and healthcare landscape plays a role in discovering what you can do now to make financial choices for your future.

Remember, every small step taken today, even just in mindset, can lead to significant financial gains tomorrow. Equip yourself with the right tools and mindset, make informed decisions, and watch your ability to strengthen your financial mindset over time.

Affirmation #4:
I am paid abundantly. I have access to multiple sources of income that support my lifestyle of freedom.

FREE NURSE ACTION CHECKLIST: MANAGING YOUR MONEY LIKE A FREE NURSE

1. **Bust the Myth.**
   ☐ Say it out loud: "I don't have to wait for a raise to build wealth."

☐ Ask yourself: Am I putting too much power in someone else's hands—like my boss or hospital—to fix my
finances?

2. **Check Your Mindset.**

☐ Do I believe my paycheck is my ceiling—or my launchpad?

☐ Affirm: "I am paid abundantly and multiply my income
through smart choices."

3. **Track It to Tame It.**

☐ Download a free budgeting app like Empower and connect all your accounts.

☐ Review your top three spending categories. Are they
aligned with your values?

4. **Start Building Your Safety Net.**

☐ Open a High-Yield Savings Account (HYSA)—even if
you only deposit $25/month.

☐ Set an auto-transfer to build your three-month emergency fund.

5. **Use Credit Like a Wealthy Nurse.**

☐ Apply for a rewards card that fits your lifestyle (Amazon,
Citi Double Cash, Costco).

☐ Set up autopay to avoid interest and earn cashback for
your everyday purchases.

6. **Pay Off Debt Strategically.**

☐ Make a list of all debts and interest rates.

☐ Focus on paying off the highest interest first—or transfer balances to 0% interest cards.

7. **Maximize the Free Money.**
   - ☐ Check if your job offers a 401(k) match—and contribute enough to get it.
   - ☐ Ask your HR team if you qualify for an HSA or FSA and set your monthly contribution.

8. **Start Your Personal Wealth Engine.**
   - ☐ Open a Roth or traditional IRA and set up monthly contributions.
   - ☐ Consider starting a Custodial IRA if your child has earned income.

9. **Stay in the Game.**
   - ☐ Schedule a 15-minute weekly money check-in.
   - ☐ Make it enjoyable: coffee, music, candles—whatever keeps you consistent.

CHAPTER 5

INVESTING IN THE STOCK MARKET

Myth #5:
The stock market is just gambling.

What if I told you the stock market saved my nursing career? As a psychiatric mental health nurse with over 18 years of experience, I've always been committed to my calling despite the inherent risks. A far too common occurrence, at least one-third of healthcare workers are assaulted during their careers. Often underreported, nurses and healthcare workers put themselves in harm's way every day to selflessly care for patients, their families, and their communities.

The patient assault I experienced marked a particularly dark moment for me, compounded by my past as a survivor of domestic violence and an abusive marriage.

I returned to therapy and worked through once again the trauma and embarrassment of being victimized. It was an important move and catapulted me into a trajectory of discovery. I'm grateful I was strong enough to recognize the opportunity to move forward.

This is an investment chapter for nurses, not hospital and societal reform. But for a moment, imagine a world where nurses have ready access to build wealth, have fulfilling relationships, and live a healthy lifestyle that helps them face nursing challenges head-on. While fulfilling their calling, they would have a clear roadmap to personal freedom—financial, relationship, spiritual, and health freedom.

Burnout rates are alarmingly high, and the need for more nurses remains critical. Would nursing shortages become a thing of the past as more individuals were attracted to the profession?

As discussed in the last chapter, nurses will never be paid what they are worth. Even though they should be, it's just pure economics. More than that, nursing is not a profession that should ever have been monetized. But it's what we have right now, so what is my mission? To revolutionize nursing by bringing us back to our roots using the tools at our current disposal.

It was during my downtime recovering from the assault that I had a realization: my financial security needed to be as resilient as my commitment to healthcare or any career. It's not just about earning a salary; it's about creating multiple income streams and securing a stable financial future when you can't or don't want to work. It's how the wealthy have always done it and how nurses will do it.

Initially, I dabbled in the stock market without much direction. I was used to taking risks. I have purchased rental properties in Oregon, Puerto Rico, and Montana, which carry considerable risk but have been quite profitable. On the other hand, the stock market was uncharted territory, and I had many limiting beliefs to overcome.

I'll give you my Nurse's Guide to Freedom Boosting Investing in this chapter. But credit must go where credit is due because these investing gems come from The Invest Diva Kiana Danial. Who or what is an Invest Diva or Invest Divo? Put simply, it's a movement that I discovered in December 2022.

Kiana Danial founded Invest Diva as a financial education platform that empowers individuals, particularly high-level professionals, to invest and manage their financial portfolios confidently. The platform provides training and tools to help users from all backgrounds understand and engage in various forms of investing, including stocks, Forex, and cryptocurrencies.

Invest Diva offers a range of online courses, one-on-one coaching, and detailed investment analysis to demystify the complex world of finance and make investing accessible to everyone.

With a strong focus on risk management and strategic financial planning, Invest Diva has cultivated a diverse and vibrant community of members across more than 130 countries. This global reach underscores the universal appeal and effectiveness of their educational content and investing philosophy.

This company not only educated me about investing but also provided the tools and confidence I needed to take control of my financial future. Within a year of following their guidance, I built a portfolio worth nearly $60,000, a $6,000 IRA, and $7,000 in cryptocurrencies.

After 18 months, I had a six-figure portfolio, making $1000/ month in dividends. I've doubled my nursing income, retired my father and mother, supported family on their career path, own $2 million in assets, and have a net worth of $1.3 million. And I'm just a regular old bedside nurse at heart. I've learned an overwhelming amount from Kiana and her money coaches, and I couldn't be more grateful.

For you to fully benefit from what I'm doing in the stock market, it's crucial to have a coach and mentor to help you get started. Take this chapter to heart because this is where the magic happens!

THE NURSE'S GUIDE TO FREEDOM-BOOSTING INVESTING: 10 RULES FOR SWEET SUCCESS

Rule #1: Patience is a profitable virtue.

One of the reasons why people are afraid to invest in the stock market is because of the horror stories they hear about traders losing it all. Trading is a very risky business. What I'm doing and what Invest Diva teaches is not trading, it's long-term value investing.

I never knew the difference until I learned it from Kiana. Trading and long-term investing represent two fundamentally different approaches to participating in the financial markets, each with distinct strategies, goals, and tax implications.

Trading involves buying and selling stocks, bonds, or other securities frequently, often within the same day or over a few days or weeks, to capitalize on short-term market fluctuations. Traders seek to maximize immediate returns, often at the cost of higher risk and greater transaction fees.

In contrast, long-term investing involves holding onto securities for extended periods, typically years or even decades, to benefit from long-term growth in the value of these investments through market cycles.

One significant advantage of long-term investing is the favorable tax treatment of long-held investments. When stocks or other securities are held for more than one year before being sold, any gains are considered long-term capital gains. These are taxed at lower rates than short-term gains, which are taxed as ordinary income at rates as high as 37%. Long-term capital gains are taxed at 0%, 15%, or 20%, depending on your taxable income.

This tax advantage helps preserve more of your investment gains and also encourages the practice of "buy and hold," reducing market volatility and promoting more stability in investment portfolios. This approach aligns well with building wealth over time, taking advantage of compounding returns, and reducing the impact of taxes on your overall investment growth.

Rule #2: There is risk in everything.

Let me say it again, there is risk in everything. For example, if you don't invest, you risk letting your money become a victim of inflation or spending it. If you leave it in the bank, you risk losing interest from market gains compared to low savings rates. If you invest in a college career, you risk not using that degree or not making money while in school. If you decide to rent and not buy a house, you risk losing out on property appreciation.

When you realize there is risk in everything, you start weighing your risk more carefully and learn your risk tolerance. Risk tolerance refers to an individual's capacity and willingness to endure declines in the value of their investments in exchange for potentially higher returns.

It is a psychological trait that influences financial decision-making. Learning your risk tolerance, which is typically described as low, medium, or high, is key to understanding your investment strategy.

Your risk tolerance can change over time, so it's not a set-it-and-forget-it sort of thing. You reevaluate periodically with income changes and life events. When you take Invest Diva's Triple Compounding Masterclass, you will learn about your individual risk tolerance.

Rule #3: The market is rooted in psychology, not math.

One of the most astounding concepts about investing that intrigued me as a mental health nurse was learning that the stock market is more about psychology than math.

For any asset that has value, its worth is determined by market sentiment. Put more plainly, if people believe an asset has worth, it does. Crazy huh? Going back to Chapter 1, it's all about beliefs!

Once you understand this psychology, you learn what prices to buy and sell stocks at. Market sentiment creates key psychological levels that investors will not allow the price to push past. And you begin to learn what you value and what lows or highs you are willing to buy and sell at.

For any stock you are considering selling, ask yourself, "If I sold this today and the market price went up, how would I feel?" Or

"If I didn't sell and the market price went down, how would I feel?" Which feeling feels worse? You pick the one that feels less gut-wrenching and have your answer as to whether you should sell. Very little math in that. Kiana calls these her "Compass Confidence" questions, and they work!

Rule #4: Pick assets that you have already invested in.

Confidence in your assets is crucial to maintaining a steady investment strategy and avoiding impulsive decisions driven by market fluctuations. Fear of missing out (FOMO) and panic selling are common emotional responses that can disrupt even the most thought-out investment plans. FOMO can lead investors to make hasty purchases based on others' actions or market hype, potentially buying at peaks.

Conversely, panic selling typically occurs during market downturns, when investors sell their assets in fear of further losses, often missing the opportunity for potential recovery and gains.

Building confidence in your investment choices through thorough research and a clear understanding of each asset's long-term potential is essential. This approach helps mitigate the risks associated with emotional investing and reinforces the discipline needed to adhere to your financial goals, regardless of market volatility.

Choose companies you believe in, already use, and invest in by buying their products. Companies that you feel contribute to society in a way that aligns with your values and that you can see yourself sticking with through the hard times. Category kings like Amazon, Apple, Google, Meta, and Microsoft, just to name a few, are typically stocks that can weather the storms of recession and the tides of global change.

Rule #5: Passive income from dividends, yes, please!

There is something purely sexy about dividend investing, earning money with minimal effort involved. It's certainly nothing new, but it was very new to me.

I remember exactly where I was when I earned my first dividend.

I was in a hotel room, waiting for my new condo to close. Everything I owned was packed away in boxes, my future was in limbo, and I was obsessively refreshing my Robinhood app to pass the time and ease the nerves.

Then, there it was—$0.60. Not a typo. Sixty cents. From Starbucks.

I had scraped together just enough money—$100—to buy 1.137656 shares. It felt almost silly. I couldn't even afford two shares of the company. Just one … and some change.

But that 60 cents? It felt like gold. It was the first time money had shown up for me without me clocking in, breaking a sweat, or being on call.

It was small, sure. But it was proof. Proof that my money could work even when I wasn't. Proof that maybe—just maybe—freedom wasn't as far away as I thought.

You want to know the wild part? That $100 I put into Starbucks—one of the most beloved (and overpriced) coffee shops on the planet—was about the same cost as twelve grande lattes. I had basically bought myself the equivalent of a "forever coffee." Not in caffeine, but in income.

I went from being a lifelong Starbucks consumer to becoming a part-owner of Starbucks.

And let me tell you, coffee hits different when you own the company.

That tiny dividend shifted something inside me. It taught me that I didn't need thousands to get started. I just needed to get started.

The sixty cents wasn't the real dividend. The belief I gained in myself was.

IF YOU CAN MAKE SIXTY CENTS, YOU CAN MAKE SIX THOUSAND

Dividends are payments made by a corporation to its shareholders, representing a portion of the company's earnings distributed as a reward for their investment. Typically issued by well-established and financially stable companies, dividends can be paid out in cash or as additional shares of stock.

The company's board of directors usually decides them, and they can be distributed quarterly, semi-annually, or annually, depending on the company's dividend policy. The amount of each dividend payment is determined per share, so the total dividend an investor receives depends on the number of shares they own.

Dividends are attractive to investors because they provide a steady income stream and can reflect the company's confidence in its financial health and ongoing profitability. For many, especially retirees or those seeking a consistent income from their investments, dividends are a critical aspect of their investment strategy, offering the benefits of regular earnings while still providing potential for capital appreciation.

Dividend investing offers notable tax advantages, making it an attractive option for building wealth through consistent income streams. One of the key benefits is the favorable tax treatment of qualified dividends compared to nonqualified dividends.

Qualified dividends are paid by U.S. corporations or qualifying foreign companies and must meet specific criteria set by the IRS. These dividends are taxed at the lower long-term capital gains tax rates of 0%, 15%, or 20%, depending on your taxable income and filing status. This rate is significantly lower than the ordinary income tax rates, which can go as high as 37%.

In contrast, nonqualified dividends are taxed as ordinary income. These typically include dividends on shares held for less than the required 60 days within the 121-day period that begins 60 days before the ex-dividend date.

Also, dividends from certain foreign entities and special dividends determined by the IRS as nonqualified fall into this category. The higher tax rate on nonqualified dividends makes it essential for investors to consider their holding periods and the source of their dividend income to optimize their tax liability.

For my Sweet 16 Dividend Plan, go to www.freenurses.co/sweet-16, which gives you my top current dividend stock recommendations that have complemented my portfolio perfectly.

Rule #6: Compounding is the eighth wonder of the world.

Compounding is often hailed as the eighth wonder of the world, a testament to its profound impact on wealth accumulation. This financial principle involves the process where the earnings from an asset are reinvested to generate their own earnings.

Over time, compounding can significantly increase the value of an initial investment without requiring additional capital contributions, as the returns from the original amount generate further returns.

Let's look at an example nurses can relate to: Bacterial Growth.

Imagine a single bacterium placed in a nutrient-rich culture medium at 8 a.m. Suppose this bacterium has a doubling time of just 20 minutes, meaning every 20 minutes, each bacterium divides into two.

Here's how the growth might look:

- At 8:20 a.m., there are two bacteria.
- At 8:40 a.m., there are four bacteria.
- At 9 a.m., there are eight bacteria, and so on.

By midday, the exponential growth due to compounding (in this case, the bacteria doubling) becomes very apparent:

- By 12 p.m., assuming no limitations on space or resources, the number has grown to over 16 million bacteria, starting from just one.

This example illustrates how something small can grow exponentially in a predictable pattern, much like investments growing due to compound interest. By consistently investing and allowing earnings to compound, investors can exponentially increase their wealth, setting a strong foundation for long-term financial security. This makes compounding not just a tool for growth but a fundamental strategy for anyone aiming to achieve and sustain financial independence.

Rule #7: Your financial freedom number

Calculating your financial freedom number is an essential step toward achieving financial independence. It represents the money you must invest to cover your living expenses indefinitely. Here's a straightforward method to calculate this important figure so you know what is achievable:

1. **Determine your annual expenses**: Start by calculating how much you spend each year. Include all your expenses, such as housing, food, healthcare, transportation, entertainment, insurance, and any other recurring expenses.

2. **Choose a safe withdrawal rate**: A common guideline is the "4% rule," which suggests you can withdraw 4% of your investment portfolio each year to cover your living expenses without depleting your principal over time. This rule assumes a balance between stocks and bonds that can sustain such withdrawals, considering inflation and investment returns.

3. **Calculate your financial freedom number**: Divide your annual expenses by your chosen withdrawal rate. For example, if your annual expenses are $50,000, you would divide this by 0.04 (or 4%).

Financial Freedom Number is $50,000/.04
= $1,250,000

You would need $1,250,000 invested to cover your expenses indefinitely without having to work or exhausting your funds. This number provides a target for your savings and investment plan to achieve financial freedom.

While $1.25 million might seem a long way from where you are now, it's not that much either. With all the talk of millions and millions of dollars every day in the news, all you might need is 1.25 of them, and you are free. By using compounding and the principles taught with Invest Diva, you can potentially accelerate that growth even more.

Rule #8: Don't put all your eggs in one basket.

Diversification is a fundamental investment strategy that involves spreading your investments across various financial instruments, industries, and other categories to reduce exposure to any particular asset or risk. The core idea behind diversification is to minimize the risk of a major loss to your overall portfolio by allocating investments among diverse assets.

For example, if you owned stocks that were only in the technology sector in 2022, your portfolio likely took a significant hit. Tech had a particularly rough year that year, with the Dow Jones U.S. Technology Index, an index tracking major tech companies, down more than 35%.

The NASDAQ, another tech-focused index, was down over 33%. This was partly due to rising inflation and interest rates, which affected their companies' bottom lines. Tech started cutting jobs, which impacted investor confidence.

In addition, the war in Russia started, and there was fear of recession. However, if you were also invested in property, your property values nearly doubled. This would have acted as a hedge for your investment losses, making it less likely that you would need to sell anything at a loss. Other common hedges to encourage diversification are:

- **Gold and precious metals**: Investing in gold or other precious metals can hedge against inflation and currency devaluation. Gold often moves inversely to the stock market and is seen as a safe haven during economic uncertainty.

- **Crypto:** Using cryptocurrency as a hedge is an increasingly popular strategy among investors looking to diversify their portfolios beyond traditional assets like stocks, bonds, and precious metals due to its decentralization and technology.

- **Using ETFs and Mutual Funds**: Certain ETFs and mutual funds are designed to hedge against various risks. For example, inverse ETFs aim to earn gains from stock declines by shorting stocks, which is suitable for hedging against market downturns.

- **Asset Allocation**: Adjusting the mix of asset classes (e.g., shifting from stocks to bonds or vice versa) based on market conditions or risk tolerance can act as a hedge. More conservative assets like bonds provide income and lower volatility, offering protection in downturns.

Insurance is critical. Life insurance isn't just about protection—it's about strategy. Many nurses, including myself, have taken it a step further by becoming licensed insurance agents. Why? Because once you understand how insurance works, you realize it's not just a safety net—it's a wealth-building tool.

One powerful option is indexed universal life insurance (IUL), a type of permanent life insurance that combines a death benefit with a cash value account tied to a stock market index.

IULs offer the potential for growth during market upswings, with a 0% guaranteed floor—meaning your policy won't lose value due to a market downturn. While this isn't the same as a guaranteed return, it's a built-in safety feature that protects your principal.

You can also borrow against the policy's cash value, giving you access to liquid funds when needed—for emergencies, investment opportunities, or even your dream vacation. It's one of the best long-term financial planning tools I've seen.

Not everyone needs a permanent policy right away. Term life insurance is a great, affordable option for nurses just starting out. It gives you pure protection for a set period (like 10, 20, or 30 years) and brings peace of mind at a price that works with your budget.

Whether you use life insurance for personal protection or turn it into a side hustle like I'm doing, understanding how it works is one more way to secure your financial future and help others do the same.

I chose to partner with Virtuity because their mission matches everything I'm building here with Free Nurses. Like me, they believe financial literacy is the cornerstone of freedom. They don't just sell policies—they help people understand and harness the financial power of insurance for legacy, leverage, and long-term security.

Ready to learn how insurance can fit into your financial freedom plan? **Go to thefreenurses.com/insurance-for-nurses** to get started.

Rule #9: Believe that you can.

Self-belief is the cornerstone of successful investing. It's not just about having the resources; it's about trusting your ability to manage and grow those resources. Many nurses may feel hesitant about stepping into the world of investing due to uncertainties or a lack of financial education. Even just the terminology might leave you feeling overwhelmed.

However, embracing a mindset of growth and confidence is crucial. If you can make it through nursing school and do what you do every day as a nurse, saving lives and healing patients with intelligence, technology, and compassion, you can do this.

Remember, every expert was once a beginner. Education, whether through courses, books, or seminars like those offered by Invest Diva, builds your financial literacy, empowering you to make informed decisions.

Believing in yourself also means recognizing that you can navigate the ups and downs of investing by applying sound principles and seeking advice when needed. This belief is what transforms doubts into decisive actions toward financial independence.

Rule #10: Do it now.

Procrastination is a common barrier to financial freedom. Kiana Danial says, "The best time to invest was 20 years ago. The second-best time is now." Many people miss out on precious time, fearing that they can't afford to invest, worrying they will make a mistake or lose it all.

Delaying your investment not only costs you in terms of compounding returns but also in the invaluable learning experiences that come with being actively involved in the markets.

Begin with small, manageable steps, like setting aside a portion of your paycheck for investment or starting with low-risk assets. Use tools and resources available to you to demystify the process. The longer you wait, the more you miss the opportunity to grow your wealth.

By starting now, you take control of your financial future, ensuring that you are working toward securing your immediate needs and your goal of being a Free Nurse. Remember, the journey to financial freedom begins with a single step. Make that step today and keep building on it consistently.

CULTIVATING AN ABUNDANCE MINDSET—$25,000 LESSONS FROM A CEO

In healthcare, where the pressures of life-or-death decisions and high-stress environments can weigh heavily on one's spirit, nurses need to nurture an abundance mindset. This chapter draws upon the insights of Kiana Danial, CEO of Invest Diva and *New York Times* Best Seller, who is frequently invited on Fox and CNN for her investing wisdom.

Imagine being 18, leaving your homeland of Iran, and venturing alone to Japan to study electrical engineering—all in Japanese. Kiana Danial did just that. As the only woman and foreigner in her classes, she faced immense challenges, earning her degree and even appearing on Japanese television.

In 2008, during the global financial crisis, Kiana made an unexpected profit by trading currencies, igniting her passion for investing. This newfound interest led her to Wall Street, where she secured a job at a Forex brokerage.

Her innovative ideas were met with resistance, and she was ultimately fired. To compound the setback, her relationship ended shortly after, leaving her jobless and heartbroken in New York City.

Determined not to be defeated, Kiana immersed herself in financial education, learning everything she could about investing. She realized the financial world was often intimidating and inaccessible, especially for women.

This realization inspired her to create Invest Diva in 2012—a platform that empowers women to take control of their financial futures.

Through Invest Diva, Kiana has transformed her life and the lives of countless others. She built a multimillion-dollar portfolio and became a best-selling author, all while helping women worldwide achieve financial independence.

Kiana's story is a testament to resilience and the power of self-belief. She turned adversity into opportunity and now serves as a mentor to many, including me. Kiana charges $25,000/hour as a speaker, and you are getting this information for the cost of my book. Cha-ching. Enjoy the abundance that follows!

Understanding Abundance

What does it mean to possess abundance? "The definition of abundance is your ability to do what you need to do when you need to do it," Kiana says. This perspective shifts the focus from a purely materialistic view of abundance to one that values freedom and capability.

For nurses, this means having the resources—emotional, intellectual, and financial—to provide care and make decisions that are best for their patients and themselves.

Abundance is about being able to offer value through one's actions: "In order to make money, I actually have to offer value to people who need it and then offer it in their specific way." Nurses provide immense value through their skills and compassion under challenging and unstable conditions. They are the Swiss Army knives of healthcare—talk about abundance! In just one shift, they're patching you up, tweaking your diet, and even tending to your mental wellness. All that in one go! It's like having a gourmet chef, a personal therapist, and a superhero all rolled into one, armed with bandages, IVs, and snacks, ready to tackle whatever comes through the hospital doors.

Who can put a price tag on that? "Money can buy health, travel, experiences, and a lot of amazing things, and whatever you feel that you need to do to go to your next level that money can buy, but give money to a person on their deathbed and it is of no use," Kiana says.

The Role of Money in Abundance

While money is a crucial tool, it's just one aspect of abundance. Kiana points out, "There's so much money out there. There's an abundance of money. It's endless." Having this abundant and positive mindset about money will help you see it in its place as something that's easy to get. "Money is a tool; it is a form of energy that makes 99% of things happen."

While financial resources are necessary, they are not sufficient to address every need, especially the most profound human experiences—compassion, presence, and empathy—that nurses provide. So, nurses are a step ahead of the game. Because they have created so much nonfinancial abundance already, they are in a prime position to receive money, one of the easiest forms of abundance to obtain.

"In order to make a lot of money, you have to stop thinking about yourself and start thinking about others and what they need." Nurses' focus on service aligns naturally with the concept of abundance through service. Then why don't they have more money?

The Power of Giving and Receiving

A significant part of abundance involves the balance between giving and receiving. Kiana emphasizes the joy derived from giving: "When you help a patient, and you know that that patient is not necessarily directly paying you, how does that make you feel?"

For many nurses, the emotional and spiritual rewards of caring for others keep them committed and focused. However, Kiana also stresses the importance of being open to receiving, whether it's support, gratitude, or compensation. "Receiving is also abundance." Recognizing one's worth and being receptive to abundance is crucial for personal and professional well-being. Nurses should balance their natural propensity for giving with openness to receiving, recognizing it as a form of abundance. "You need to understand that if these patients were not open to receiving your gift, you wouldn't experience the amazing

feelings that are immeasurable by any symbol of money or anything else." So, allow yourself to enjoy your profession more.
Don't fight it and open up to receiving.

The Influence of Mindset

These views on money, giving and receiving, and abundance
will begin to shape your mindset. Abundance isn't just about
accumulating wealth but also about enjoying a rich quality of
life that a positive, expansive mindset supports. Viewing your
professional landscape not as limited but as ripe with opportunities for growth, learning, and financial gain will take you further than you could imagine. Here are some additional practical
steps toward creating abundance in your life:

- **Cultivate Gratitude**: Recognize and appreciate every
  small win and positive moment in your day. This practice elevates your mood and will help you recognize the
  abundance already in your life.

- **Educate Yourself Financially**: Just like you are doing
  now! You are probably beginning to realize that you
  cannot be financially abundant without a positive view
  of money.

- **Engage in Lifelong Learning**: Continuous professional development ensures that you remain competitive and adaptable, qualities essential for thriving in the
  ever-evolving field of healthcare. Investing in yourself is
  one of the best investments you can make.

- **Advocate for Yourself and Others**: Learn to negoti-
  ate effectively and advocate for better conditions and

pay. Recognizing your value is a crucial step in fostering an abundance mindset.

- **Network and Connect**: Building relationships within and outside your field can open up new paths for personal and professional growth, enriching your career and life in unexpected ways.

LET'S GO!

In embracing Kiana Danial's principles of abundance and investing, nurses can transform their approach to their careers and lives. By understanding the multifaceted nature of abundance—encompassing money, opportunities, relationships, and personal growth—nurses reach their wealthy free nurse status, living a freakin' awesome life while helping others live theirs.

Ultimately, cultivating an abundance mindset is about more than financial success; it's about enriching every aspect of one's life and career in nursing, allowing one to provide the best care possible while living a fulfilling and empowered life.

Affirmation #5:

I am abundant. Money comes to me frequently and easily. I use my money to make more money, which makes more money.

FREE NURSE ACTION CHECKLIST: BUILD WEALTH THROUGH STOCK MARKET INVESTING

1. **Bust the Myth.**
   - ☐ Say it out loud: "The stock market is mental—not money."
   - ☐ Reflect: What belief is keeping me from investing confidently?

2. **Start Small and Start Now.**
   - ☐ Open a brokerage account (Robinhood, Fidelity, or your platform of choice).
   - ☐ Invest in one company you believe in—even if it's just $10.

3. **Get Your First Win.**
   - ☐ Buy a dividend-paying stock (like Starbucks) and watch that first payout come in.
   - ☐ Celebrate it—even if it's $0.60. That's the start of your compounding journey.

4. **Learn the Game.**
   - ☐ Take the **Free Triple Compounding Masterclass** at www.freenurses.co/tcs.
   - ☐ Learn the difference between long-term investing and trading.

5. **Know Your Risk.**
   - ☐ Complete a risk tolerance quiz (Invest Diva includes this).
   - ☐ Choose assets that match your personality and peace of mind.

6. Think Long-Term.

☐ Set your **financial freedom number** (Annual expenses ÷ 0.04).

☐ Journal what life would look like if you hit that number.

7. Diversify Like a Boss.

☐ Review your investments: Are they all in one basket?

☐ Add a dividend stock, an ETF, or a different sector.

8. Embrace Your Worth.

☐ Affirm: "I am smart enough to build wealth. I invest with purpose and confidence."

☐ Take the next small, brave step—every investor starts somewhere.

CHAPTER 6

BE YOUR OWN NURSE BOSS

Myth #6:
I only need one income.

This is the chapter that turns clock-punching nurses into confident nurse bosses.

When I first stepped into my role as a nurse leader, I thought I was signing up to support, educate, and advocate. I wasn't naïve—I knew leadership could be hard. But nothing could have prepared me for what came next.

Before COVID even reached our hospital doors, our team was already breaking apart. Toxic behaviors—gossip, resentment, distrust—had taken root. Leadership had made mistakes. I had made mistakes. All of it laid the groundwork for a firestorm. And then came the gasoline: the way our unionizing efforts unfolded.

I wasn't against unions. I believed, and still do, that nurses deserve a voice. But what I witnessed devastated me. Instead of banding together, our team splintered into two. Lies spread.

Friendships dissolved. People who had once shared laughter in the breakroom now couldn't even make eye contact. It broke my heart. This wasn't what I signed up for. And because I was in a leadership role, I was automatically on the wrong side.

And then, just when I thought it couldn't get worse, COVID hit.

Suddenly, union meetings and workplace politics fell away. We were thrust onto the frontlines of a global pandemic, fighting an invisible enemy we didn't understand. Nurses and healthcare workers became warriors, battling exhaustion, fear, and a disease that didn't play by any of the rules we knew.

The chaos was relentless. Policies changed weekly. Fear lived in the air with us—thick and heavy. For the first time in my career, it wasn't just the patients who were terrified—it was us.

We swabbed weekly, waiting for the dreaded positive test that would send us into quarantine—and leave our teams even more short-staffed. Staffing the unit and the hospital became a daily act of insanity.

I'll never forget the day I became one of the first nurses in the nation to be vaccinated. We volunteered to be human guinea pigs because we knew we had to lead by example, and it was also a relief to have something that might protect us. It was a proud, hopeful, and sobering moment. I was tearful afterward—not for myself, but for our world.

Those three years in leadership weren't about climbing a ladder. They were about survival. Leadership didn't make me feel powerful—it made me feel exhausted, scared, and small.

But it also forged something in me that I could never have learned in a classroom.

I realized I wasn't a born leader in the traditional sense. I didn't crave power. I still prefer teaching, mentoring, and inspiring, not corrective action and enforcing rules. But through the crucible of crisis, I learned something much deeper: how to be my own boss.

I learned how to lead myself even when I was tired. How to make decisions even when there were no good ones. How to stand up for others even when it cost me personally. How to build something out of the ashes when everything around me burned down.

I know now that I was in that role for a reason. It wasn't to make a name for myself. It was to prepare me for a bigger mission—helping nurses and my family reclaim their finances, their joy, and their lives. Because bosses aren't born. They're built.

After becoming a boss in a world on fire, I knew one thing for sure:

One income is never enough. One plan is never enough. Redundancy isn't optional—it's protection. The smartest nurses didn't just survive COVID—they had exit strategies.

THE REALITY OF MULTIPLE INCOME STREAMS

Most of us were taught by our parents, school, and societal norms that we only need one income, one career, or one job. The reality is quite different. Think about your situation. Are you a single mom with two jobs? Do both you and your partner work to make ends meet? Are you working more than 36 hours per week as a nurse, picking up extra shifts? If you said yes to any of these questions, you know that having just one income source is not sustainable. Why is that?

A report from the Pew Research Center indicates that in many dual-income households, both partners must work not just for financial stability but to maintain a desirable standard of living. The Federal Reserve's Report on the Economic Well-Being of U.S. Households in 2020 found that nearly a quarter of adults engaged in gig work or other forms of income diversification to supplement their earnings.

The gap becomes even more obvious when you look at how the wealthy build and protect their finances. It's no secret that most millionaires don't rely on just one paycheck—they diversify.

The widely quoted idea that millionaires have seven income streams isn't based on a single study, but the pattern holds true across countless financial experts, interviews, and case studies. These income sources often include real estate, investments, side businesses, intellectual property, and more. The goal? Security and flexibility.

Meanwhile, many of us were raised to believe that one good, stable job should cover all our needs. That mindset is outdated. In today's economy, relying on a single source of income is not just risky—it's a liability. Wealthy people have known this for centuries.

Specific to nursing, the trend of pursuing multiple income streams is gaining traction. While direct statistics on nurses operating with multiple income sources are sparse, anecdotal evidence suggests a significant shift. Many nurses are turning to side hustles, from freelance healthcare writing and consulting to starting their own health-related businesses. This entrepreneurial spirit not only bolsters financial growth but also enhances professional fulfillment and career longevity.

Meet Michelle: The Nurse Who Had to Start Over

Michelle had been a nurse for 23 years.

She could place an IV in her sleep, de-escalate a Code Gray with a single look, and knew every trick for calming a panicked family member without saying a word. People came to her for answers. Students wanted to shadow her. Doctors trusted her.

But Michelle hadn't trusted *herself* in a long time.

She was 49, newly divorced, and freshly displaced from the charge role she'd held for nearly a decade. The unit was changing. Younger nurses were faster with the tech. Administration wanted "fresh energy." No one had said it out loud, but Michelle felt it in her bones: *You're being quietly replaced.*

At home, her kids were off at college, her fridge mostly empty, and her evenings unbearably quiet. She had spent so many years giving—at work, home, and church—that she didn't know who she was anymore when she finally had time to herself.

So she filled her days with extra shifts. Not because she needed the money, but because she didn't know what else to do.

Until one day, a young nurse she'd precepted years before returned to the unit to visit. They caught up in the breakroom, and when Michelle asked what she was doing now, the answer knocked the wind out of her.

"Oh, I'm still nursing part-time. But I run retreats for burned-out healthcare workers now. Mindfulness, meditation, nature therapy—it's my own business. I made more last month than I did in three months full-time."

Michelle stared at her, stunned.

"Wait. You *what?*"

They talked for 45 minutes. When the younger nurse left, Michelle just sat there, her lukewarm coffee forgotten.

She had never seen herself as an entrepreneur. She barely saw herself as *relevant* anymore. But in that conversation, a switch flipped.

That night, she dusted off a notebook she hadn't touched in years. She started writing—not charting, but dreaming. Ideas, goals, little whispers of possibility. She looked into health coaching. Signed up for a free webinar. Then a course. Then a mentorship program.

Within a year, Michelle launched a part-time consulting business helping nurses transition into leadership without losing their sanity. She spoke at a conference. She got paid for her wisdom—for her scars. And she realized: this next chapter was hers to write.

She hadn't missed the boat. She *was* the boat.

Today, Michelle still works per diem. But she doesn't *need* to. She chooses to. Because she finally believes what everyone else knew all along: Her experience wasn't something to retire. It was something to *build on.*

THE FIRST PLACE TO LOOK FOR EXTRA CASH—YOUR TAXES!

We discussed in Chapter 3 how the tax laws benefit anything that makes the government wealthier and protects its interests. You've learned that the government is a business, and business owners are one of the main categories it incentivizes.

Besides housing, your biggest expense as a nurse is taxes! Starting a business can help save those hard-earned nursing wages. Instead of paying the government in taxes, the government pays you to do what you love (if you've chosen the right kind of business for yourself) by lowering your tax bill.

It can be a beautiful symbiotic relationship once you figure it out. Maybe beautiful isn't the right word, but you get my point. It's pretty sweet. It's important to note that this is not cheating the government. This is receiving legitimate tax deductions and credits in exchange for building something that supports an economy in which you participate.

Preston Anderson, whom I introduced in Chapter 3, further unveils the often misunderstood purpose of the tax code—not as a mere tool for revenue but as a means for behavior modification through incentives and penalties.

"The tax code is about behavior modification," Preston explains, shedding light on how the government uses fiscal policies to influence public actions rather than merely collecting dues. He articulates how understanding and leveraging these aspects can lead to significant savings.

He emphasizes the disparity between public perception and the reality of the tax code's intentions, highlighting that the complexity arises from efforts to maintain fairness through detailed regulations shaped by various lobbying interests. This complexity, while daunting, opens avenues for substantial savings if navigated wisely.

This same perspective is available to all nurses navigating the complexities of personal and professional finances. For instance, the government incentivizes retirement savings by offering deductions for contributions while imposing penalties for premature withdrawals.

Similarly, credits are available for eco-friendly purchases like electric cars, demonstrating how strategic financial activities can align with tax benefits. This narrative not only demystifies tax codes but also encourages nurses to engage proactively with their finances, transforming their approach from passive participants to informed stakeholders in their financial well-being.

Through Preston's insights, nurses are invited to view tax planning not just as a seasonal chore but as a strategic element of their overall financial health, capable of delivering tangible benefits beyond mere compliance into substantial economic empowerment. This shift in perspective, from dread to proactive engagement, is a powerful tool for financial freedom that resonates deeply within the nursing community.

Preston helped me bring this refreshing perspective on tax planning to my business. In my experience, a single consultation with Preston enabled me to reclaim $37,000 on my taxes—an empowering moment that underscores the value of knowledgeable guidance in tax planning.

For example, in 2023, I earned $226,434 as a nurse working on average 50-60 hours/week. These wages included incentives, bonuses, and crisis pay. I initially paid a whopping $37,867 in federal taxes and $13,518 in state taxes. I also earned approximately $10k in capital gains, interest, and dividends.

If I did not have a business, I would have said goodbye to over $50k in taxes, but I have one that handles property rentals and runs my business, Free Nurses. I received $10,119 back from the state and $27,530 from the federal government, which left me paying only $10,337 in federal taxes and $3,399 for state taxes. That's about a 1.5% state tax and a 4.5% federal rate. This does not include other taxes, such as social security, property taxes, etc. It is a simplified calculation of what can be done. But you get my point, right?

The notion that some of the world's wealthiest individuals, such as Jeff Bezos, Elon Musk, Donald Trump, and Warren Buffett, pay minimal taxes often sparks controversy and highlights complex issues around tax policy and financial strategy. These prominent figures have been criticized for allegedly paying less in taxes relative to their vast fortunes.

However, their tax strategies typically involve legal avenues and financial mechanisms available within the tax code, which high-net-worth individuals often use to minimize tax liabilities.

For instance, Elon Musk and Jeff Bezos have been reported to utilize the benefits of capital gains taxes, which are lower than income taxes, by holding onto their stocks instead of selling them. This means they do not incur taxes until the assets are sold and gains are realized. Moreover, they can borrow against the value of their stock to fund their lifestyles without triggering taxable events.

Warren Buffett has famously pointed out that his effective tax rate is lower than that of his secretary, mainly because his income derives from dividends and capital gains, which are taxed at a lower rate than ordinary income.

Keep in mind that the tax rates are lower, not the tax itself. So, they are typically still paying more taxes than you, except for maybe Donald Trump. His taxes have been a subject of intense scrutiny and controversy, especially after reports surfaced that he paid only $750 in federal income taxes during certain years of his presidency. His tax returns, which involved numerous deductions, credits, and loss carryforwards, illustrate how businesses and their owners can reduce tax liabilities through depreciation and other means.

While these strategies are legal and reflect the savvy use of tax laws, they raise questions about the equity and effectiveness of the current tax code, particularly in how it benefits the wealthiest, often at the perceived expense of the middle and lower-income classes.

This underscores the importance of understanding tax laws and financial planning—it's not just for the ultra-rich; individuals at all levels can seek to optimize their tax situations with the right knowledge and strategies.

Depending on your situation, there are many opportunities to lower your tax bill. Consulting with a CPA who understands how to guide you may open your eyes. (FYI: Not all

CPAs understand how the financial system operates, so choose someone like Preston, who understands how the system was designed.) Starting a business is one such opportunity.

Meet Karina: The New Grad Who Got Derailed (Then Rerouted Herself)

Karina passed the NCLEX on her first try.

She'd dreamed of becoming a nurse since her sophomore year of high school when her little brother had a seizure in front of her, and the calmest person in the room wasn't a doctor—it was a nurse. From that moment, she was *in*. Nursing was her destiny. Her purpose. Her calling.

She finished her BSN with honors. Got her first job offer two months before graduation. Bought the stethoscope. Downloaded the apps. Watched the TikToks. She was ready.

What she wasn't ready for was what came next.

By month three, Karina was crying in the medication room.

Not because of patient care. That part she could handle. It was the politics. The side-eye from "mean girl" nurses. The nurse who rolled her eyes every time Karina asked a question. The passive-aggressive notes. The supervisor who told her to "toughen up." The patient who spit on her and the one who accused her of trying to kill him.

One night, after a brutal 12-hour shift that ended with a wrong-bed med error (thankfully caught just in time), Karina went home, curled up in bed in her scrubs, and thought: "Is this nursing? Because if it is, I don't want it."

Her dream had turned into a job she dreaded. The career she thought would light her up was draining her dry.

And then—on a random Wednesday afternoon—she came across a podcast interview with a nurse turned mindset coach who said: "The problem isn't nursing. The problem is expecting your hospital to give you meaning."

That sentence hit her like a code blue.

Karina had been waiting for the *job* to fulfill her. But maybe that wasn't the job's job.

She started journaling again. Signed up for therapy. DMed the podcast guest and asked for a book recommendation. Then another. Then another.

Within six months, Karina had completely reframed her mindset. She was still a nurse, but now she saw her job as a funding source for her real mission: becoming a mental health advocate for new grads.

She launched a tiny blog. Then a newsletter. Then a workshop series at her local nursing school called "Your Scrubs Are Not Your Self-Worth."

Karina didn't quit nursing. She *reclaimed* it. On her terms.

She's still early in her career, but her burnout didn't end her—it *birthed* her. And now she helps other new grads do the same.

Because sometimes your calling doesn't show up with fanfare.

Sometimes it shows up after you've cried in the bathroom five shifts in a row.

And sometimes, you find your strength not because the job gets easier—but because *you get clearer.*

QUESTIONS TO ASK YOURSELF TO START BRAINSTORMING ON YOUR FIRST BUSINESS

1. **Identify Your Passion:** What are you good at that also sparks joy? What takes you to your happy place? What have you always dreamed of doing that seems impossible or out of reach? This could be related to healthcare or something entirely different that you have a talent for or have always wanted to learn about.

2. **In-Demand Products and Customers:** Who can you see yourself selling something to? What can you see yourself talking about to a customer?

3. **Your Personality:** Are you an introvert or an extrovert? Is your cup filled when you socialize or when you are at home doing something yourself? Do you like writing or reading? Listening or talking? Teaching or learning?

4. **Skills:** Has anyone ever told you you were really good at something? Do you have great technical skills on the internet, computer, and smartphone? Are you more crafty and artistic? What are you proficient in? What do people ask you for advice on or come to you for answers?

5. **Your Financial Plans:** What are you planning on buying soon? What do you need right now that could be monetized?

EASY BUSINESS IDEAS TO GET YOUR FEET WET

- Do you have an extra car that you don't always use? Try renting it on Turo or a car-sharing platform. You can deduct expenses like car insurance, repairs and maintenance, and taxes. If you have been considering getting a new car, this is a great way to minimize first-year car expenses and depreciate your new asset.

- Rent out a room in your house through a short-term rental platform like VRBO or Airbnb. House expenses, repairs, and taxes will be partially deductible.

- Have you been wanting to finally start writing that first book? Take a vacation, get some inspiration for that novel, and bring it to life while roaming. Buy that new computer for your business to write and travel in style.

- Do you love giving advice or sharing ideas? Start posting on social media or YouTube and take steps to monetize your account. This will allow you to bring in passive income by posting about what you love, such as cooking, recipes, fixing cars, or some other niche others want to follow.

- Do you love to travel? Start a blog online and share tips, insights, and pictures of your travels. Travel expenses are deductible, and you can eventually monetize the blog itself.

These ideas are to get you thinking about what you are already doing. So, it doesn't have to be something new—the idea could be sitting right in front of you now.

I know two nurses who turned a guest house on their property into a cozy Airbnb. It now helps pay their mortgage. Two others got their insurance licenses—now they help families protect their futures *and* earn commission checks bigger than their hospital bonuses. Another nurse just earned her Legal Nurse Consultant certification. She's lining up her retirement with consulting gigs she can do from home in her pajamas.

WHAT IT MEANS TO MONETIZE SOMETHING

Monetizing something means creating a revenue stream from an asset, product, service, or any other resource that previously didn't generate income. This process involves finding effective ways to generate financial returns from resources that are underused or have potential market value.

Common monetization methods include advertising revenue, selling goods or services, subscription models, and licensing fees. For example, a blogger might monetize their site by adding advertisements, a software developer might monetize a free app through in-app purchases, or a company might monetize proprietary data through a subscription service.

Monetization is critical for businesses and individuals because it transforms creative, technological, and intellectual assets into viable, sustainable economic models, ultimately contributing to profitability and growth.

INVESTING AS A SIDE HUSTLE

Brian Cerezo, whom you were also introduced to, demystifies the concept of trading options as a lucrative side hustle for nurses. Brian explains, "When you think about options trading,

I don't even want to say mine is necessarily options trading because I'm only on one side of the equation."

He focuses on selling options, a strategy he considers safer and more controllable than buying options. This method involves using assets already owned, such as stocks of major companies like Apple or Nvidia, as collateral to generate income from selling call options.

Brian's approach minimizes risk while maximizing returns: "You're putting either a hundred shares up for collateral or a hundred shares worth of cash up for collateral to a specific stock ... In doing so, the market will pay you money to do it."

He describes the potential to "triple dip" on investments by earning dividends, appreciating stock values, and collecting premiums from sold options. This strategy leverages existing investments and also capitalizes on the inherent volatility and growth potential of tech stocks, making it particularly appealing.

Brian highlights the control this strategy affords: "I think the selling side is the safest because you have 90% control over what happens. You can choose the strike price and the date you would potentially want this to expire." He is cautious during volatile market conditions, such as elections or earnings reports, adapting his strategy to safeguard his investments against undue risks.

A pivotal moment in Brian's journey was the realization that options trading could serve as a substantial income stream, allowing him to generate initial capital for real estate investments.

He describes this realization as a game-changer, enabling him to transition from passive stock investments to active wealth accumulation. "Without the stock trading, I wouldn't have had the initial capital to get my primary house," he remarks, highlighting how diversified investment strategies can interlock to support substantial financial goals like property ownership.

For nurses considering options trading as a side hustle, Brian's method offers a structured approach to engage with the market while maintaining a primary career in healthcare. His course aims to teach these strategies, emphasizing the balance between risk management and potential returns. It provides a practical blueprint for nurses to expand their financial acumen and independence.

You can find a link to his site here: https://stan.store/freenurses.

YOU DON'T HAVE TO KNOW WHAT YOU ARE GOING TO DO, JUST START A BUSINESS

Starting a business can initially seem daunting, especially if you're unsure about its specific direction or focus. However, the flexibility inherent in the early stages of business development is a significant advantage. When you establish your first LLC, you only need to select a general category; this broad designation allows you the freedom to explore various interests under your business umbrella.

This exploration can be supported and enriched through tax-deductible expenses such as educational courses, books, masterclasses, online courses, and webinars. These resources count as market research and education expenses, which are not only beneficial for personal development but also financially advantageous for your business.

For example, my current business primarily involves property rentals, but as I've aimed to expand my knowledge and skill set, I've invested in investing and business management courses. This ongoing education has been crucial for my personal development and has also been instrumental in refining the strategic direction of my business.

I've been able to deduct trips and travel expenses because I attended conferences, worked on my properties, held retreats, and attended annual business meetings. Starting a business without a fixed plan might seem unconventional, but it opens up a pathway for learning and adaptation that can lead to more tailored and informed business strategies as you grow.

Starting an LLC

Starting a limited liability company (LLC) offers numerous benefits, especially for nurses looking to channel their professional expertise into a private venture. An LLC provides a formal structure to manage and grow your business, such as private nursing services, healthcare consulting, or wellness coaching, and it also offers personal liability protection, separating your business liabilities from your personal assets.

This is particularly valuable in healthcare, where professionals often face high risks. Additionally, an LLC can be advantageous for tax purposes, as it allows for pass-through taxation, which means profits are taxed only once at the personal income level, avoiding the double taxation commonly associated with corporations. Setting up an LLC involves choosing a business name, filing the necessary documents with your state, and paying a filing fee.

Nurses who want to start an LLC can utilize several online resources that make the process straightforward and manageable. Here are some common platforms and steps to consider:

1. **Secretary of State Website**: Each state's Secretary of State website is the primary resource for filing an LLC. The website provides specific information on the requirements, fees, and forms needed to establish an LLC in that state. Simply navigate to your state's government website and look for the business or corporate services section.

2. **Legal Document Services**:

   ○ **LegalZoom**: One of the most well-known online legal services that guides you through the process of creating an LLC. It offers packages that include filing the LLC with your state and providing customized legal documents.

   ○ **Rocket Lawyer**: This service offers LLC creation, legal advice, and customizable legal documents. They also provide an option for attorney support.

   ○ **Incfile**: Known for its affordability, Incfile helps with the LLC formation process and includes a free year of registered agent services with the initial filing.

3. **IRS Website**: After forming your LLC, you'll need an employer identification number (EIN), which you can

apply for directly on the IRS website. This is necessary for tax purposes and to open a business bank account.

4. **Online Business Services Platforms**:

   ○ **BizFilings**: Offers comprehensive services for forming an LLC, including options for managing ongoing legal compliance.

   ○ **MyCorporation**: Provides LLC formation services along with maintenance services like annual report filings and renewals.

   ○ **Northwest Registered Agent** (this is the one I use): Provides LLC formation services along with maintenance services like annual report filings and renewals: www.northwestregisteredagent.com

UTILIZE FREE BUSINESS RESOURCES LIKE THE SBDC

Starting a business doesn't mean you have to do it alone or spend a fortune on advice. One of the best-kept secrets for new nurse entrepreneurs is the **Small Business Development Center (SBDC)**. Funded by the U.S. Small Business Administration, SBDCs offer free or low-cost business mentoring, training, and resources in every state.

Whether you're just exploring business ideas or already have an LLC, SBDC advisors can help you write a business plan, understand market research, develop financial projections, and even navigate funding options.

I've personally used SBDC services and found them incredibly helpful in refining my business strategy and organizing my goals. They can help you network locally or regionally. They have helped plenty of nurses build their businesses, and it's a great place to start if you have an idea you want to suss out. Find your local SBDC at www.americassbdc.org and get connected!

A SUCCESSFUL NURSE ENTREPRENEUR

You've met several successful nurse entrepreneurs throughout this book, including one of my favorites—Savannah Arroyo, MSN, RN. Savannah entered the healthcare field straight out of high school with a strong desire to make a difference. After achieving a master's degree in nursing leadership and administration, she aspired to climb the ranks to a chief nursing officer.

However, the birth of her second daughter in 2020 shifted her priorities dramatically. Faced with the demands of their high-commitment jobs, Savannah and her husband reevaluated their work-life trajectory, realizing that their current paths wouldn't allow them the flexibility and time they desired with their growing family.

Within three years, Savannah transitioned from her full-time RN administrator position to managing her real estate investments, achieving the freedom and flexibility she sought.

Her journey was not just about building wealth but about empowering others, particularly nurses, to harness the power of their earnings and convert them into lasting legacies.

Savannah emphasizes the importance of financial literacy and having multiple streams of income. Her advice to nurses is to get very clear on their "why"—understanding the deeper reasons behind their financial goals. This clarity can drive the

2222

determination to pursue and succeed in alternative income streams, such as real estate.

By sharing her story and insights, Savannah hopes to inspire more nurses to explore real estate investing as a viable path to financial freedom and a better work-life balance. Her journey illustrates that with the proper knowledge and resources, nurses can leverage their hard-earned money to build wealth and secure their futures without waiting until retirement to enjoy the fruits of their labor.

The Nurse CEO Playbook: 10 Moves Savannah Arroyo Used to Buy Back Her Time

1. **Embrace Life Shifts for Financial Reevaluation**: Savannah stressed the importance of reassessing financial goals after major life changes, as she did after the birth of her second daughter.

2. **Pursuing Multiple Income Streams**: Highlighting the power of diversification, Savannah explained the freedom gained from multiple income sources: "I really stress having multiple streams of income because it gives you more freedom and options."

3. **Educate Yourself on Real Estate Investing**: Real estate investing was a key to her financial strategy. Savannah discussed her self-education process, saying, "Every time real estate investing would come up ... I started learning that it was one of the best ways to build wealth."

4. **Accelerate Financial Independence**: Savannah shared her rapid journey from learning about real estate

to achieving financial independence, which allowed her to leave her full-time job: "Within three years, I was able to walk away from my full-time RN administrator job."

5. **Define Your "Why"**: Understanding personal motivations is crucial. She emphasized setting clear goals: "We sat down and got very, very clear on our vision and where we wanted to be in three years."

6. **Explore Real Estate Syndications**: Savannah highlighted the benefits of syndications, pooling resources to invest in larger properties: "Real estate syndications are people pooling together their resources to buy a real estate asset like an apartment complex."

7. **Utilize Home Equity Strategically**: She discussed leveraging home equity to fund investments and maximize returns: "We were able to take out $80,000 worth of equity and use that to invest in real estate property earning 15-20%."

8. **Take Advantage of Tax Benefits in Real Estate**: The financial gains from real estate can be substantial, with benefits such as cash flow and tax deductions. Savannah noted, "We invest heavily in value-added opportunities. That does astronomical things to the numbers in multifamily real estate."

9. **Boost Financial Literacy Among Nurses**: Savannah is passionate about improving financial literacy, especially for healthcare professionals, explaining, "It becomes like a financial literacy aspect, which is why I'm so passionate about this."

10. **Leverage Retirement Accounts for Investments**:
    She advised using retirement accounts for real estate
    investments to potentially enhance returns: "You can
    direct your IRA money from a rollover IRA account
    into a self-directed IRA and use it to invest in these
    investments."

CONCLUSION

As you venture into the world of multiple income streams,
remember that the journey of being your own boss is completely reachable if you want it. Nurses make some excep-
tional business owners. And don't you think the world would
be a bit better if nurses owned more businesses? Embrace the
entrepreneurial spirit within you to build a secure and thriving future.

Affirmation #6:

I am successful because I draw positive experiences, people,
and opportunities to myself. I feel powerful and confident.
Money is positive energy that takes care of my worthy
needs and desires. I feel completely at ease receiving and
managing huge amounts of money, property, assets, and
investments every day.

FREE NURSE ACTION CHECKLIST: BE YOUR OWN NURSE BOSS

1. **Bust the Myth.**
   - ☐ Say it: "I can have multiple sources of income for the life I want."
   - ☐ Ask: Who taught me I could only earn money one way?

2. **Shift Your Mindset.**
   - ☐ Do I believe I can build something of my own?
   - ☐ Affirm: "I'm ready to create income streams that serve my freedom."

3. **Cut Your Tax Bill.**
   - ☐ Look at your last tax return—how much did you pay?
   - ☐ Book a call with a CPA who understands business.
   - ☐ Ask: What would change if I had a business?

4. **Find Your First Business Idea.**
   - ☐ List three things you love doing.
   - ☐ Choose one that could earn money.
   - ☐ Commit to exploring it this month.

5. **Take a Bold Step.**
   - ☐ Register your LLC.
   - ☐ Get your EIN (it's free at IRS.gov).
   - ☐ Open a separate bank account for your business.
   - ☐ Visit www.americassbdc.org and find your local office.

6. **Get Inspired.**

☐ Watch interviews of Savannah Arroyo or Brian Cerezo.

☐ Ask: What's one move I can model from their stories?

7. **Trust Yourself.**

☐ Journal: What hard thing have I already overcome?

☐ Affirm: "Bosses aren't born—they're built."

THE NURSE FREEDOM FORMULA

As you turn the final pages of this book, pause and ask yourself, "Am I living the life I envisioned as a nurse?"

If the answer stirs a desire for more—more freedom, more fulfillment, more financial security—you're ready to embark on a transformative journey with the Nurse Freedom Formula.

You now know all Six Secrets in what I call the Nurse Freedom Formula—It's time to expand your credentials beyond RN to VIPRN-Boss, where each letter represents a crucial step toward a richer life:

- **Vision and Purpose (V):** Reconnect with your why. Let your passion lead you to a fulfilling career and life.

- **Investments (I):** Make your money work as hard as you do. Secure your financial future with smart, nurse-friendly investment strategies.

- **Property (P):** Step into homeownership and test the waters of owning assets.

- **Resources/Finances (R):** Manage your finances, maximize your earnings, and manage your wealth smartly.

- **Nurse Mentor (N):** Learn from those who've navigated this path and can guide you to success.

- **Business Ownership (Boss):** Own your time, your career, and your future. Become a nurse entrepreneur.

Can you see your signature here now?

_____,VIPRN–Boss

With these credentials, you will have unlocked my Nurse Freedom Formula, which consists of six proven steps to reach the nurse life you want.

It isn't just a plan; it's a new adventure. It's a call to all nurses who feel overworked, underpaid, and undervalued—you can take control of your life and career.

It's a promise that you don't have to work exhausting shifts until retirement, miss out on life's important moments, or feel trapped in a system that doesn't value your well-being. But you might be thinking:

- I don't really have time to explore new opportunities or learn new skills with my nursing schedule and family responsibilities.

- I'm too worried about the financial risks of investing, real estate, or starting my own business. I don't want to lose money.

- It seems like a lot of work. Managing investments or running a business intimidates me because I don't have much experience in these areas.

- I'm skeptical about how the Nurse Freedom Formula can improve my life personally.

- Even though my current situation isn't ideal, I'm okay with it.

It's normal to feel apprehensive about stepping into the unknown. Change can be daunting, but it's also rewarding. Just remember, you are more than a nurse already. You are a coach, a caregiver, an educator, an advocate, a healer. You can also be a visionary, an investor, a property owner, a resourceful financier, a mentee, and a boss.

Every nurse possesses the resilience and dedication needed to master these new domains. You are already adept at managing complex challenges and caring deeply about your work—skills transferable to managing your finances, running a business, or investing in real estate.

As you implement these strategies, remember that the Nurse Freedom Formula can adapt to your personal circumstances and goals. You're not alone in this journey; a community of like-minded professionals is growing, ready to support and inspire each other.

Don't let another day pass feeling unfulfilled. Begin today by choosing one aspect of the Nurse Freedom Formula to explore further. Visit the following websites, which offer more resources daily to help you take those first confident steps.

- www.thefreenurses.com
- www.freenurse.co
- Free Triple Compounding System Masterclass: www.freenurses.co/tcs
- Triple Compounding Live Virtual Event: www.freenurses.co/tcl
- Free Nurses Stan Store: www.stan.store/freenurses
- Wealth Coaching: www.freenurses.co/nifw

Together, we can redefine what it means to be a nurse—not just in how we work, but in how we live and thrive. Let's all be independently wealthy Florence Nightingales, laser-focused on our careers and serving without worrying about finances. Let's unite to elevate our profession, enrich our lives, and ensure every nurse has the tools to succeed without financial burden.

We're changing and saving lives every day, which is some of the most important work being done on the planet. So, let's move forward with courage, armed with the knowledge and strategies from this book, to build a future where every nurse can truly say, "I am free."

Ready to begin? Head to freenurses.co/gift to grab your free gift and join the movement toward nurse freedom.

See you on the inside.

Mandie Jo, Invest Diva + Free Nurse

ACKNOWLEDGMENTS

To my parents, who read to me, played with me, and taught me to sing and love music, I want to thank you for giving me the best start in life any child could have.

To my Grama, who makes the best hash browns and gravy and was probably one of the first grandmothers to play video games with their grandchild in 1992.

To my talented, patient, and adorable brother, I think the world of you!

To love itself, which appeared in unexpected forms and helped me keep believing when I was uncertain.

To all my nurse mothers and fathers, thank you!

ABOUT THE AUTHOR

Mandie Jo has dedicated over 20 years to healthcare, specializing in psychiatric-mental health nursing. This career has not only shaped her professional life but also fueled her passion for financial and personal empowerment.

With a net worth of $1.3 million and $2 million in assets across real estate, stocks, and cryptocurrencies, Mandie has found substantial success beyond hospital corridors. She owns properties in Oregon, Montana, and Puerto Rico and has proudly retired her parents, ensuring a prosperous future for her family while continuing to serve actively in the nursing field. She was a 2024 Today's Nurse and is certified in Addictions and Psychiatric-Mental Health.

Following 11 years of committed volunteer mission work, Mandie escaped an abusive marriage in 2018 and overcame the trauma of a brutal patient assault in 2022. During the COVID-19 pandemic, she led a 40-bed inpatient psychiatric unit, steering through one of the most challenging times in modern nursing history.

Currently, Mandie travels and works as a behavioral health nurse educator specializing in workplace violence. In addition to her nursing career, she operates a thriving business designed to help nurses achieve financial independence and reclaim control over their lives. She loves the ocean and mountains, singing and playing music with her family, traveling, and being a lifelong learner.

She invites others to join her on this transformative journey, which will redefine what it means to be free and fulfilled in the nursing profession.